SEPARATION AND REUNIFICATION OF THE ELEMENTS.

Written by Spirit and Transcribed
by

Brendan O'Callaghan

I.S.M. Publications

ISBN: 9798702882765

Cover design by: Brendan O'Callaghan

Dedicated to all the stalwart warriors committed to the spiritual task of the reunification of the Elements, and restoring the Earth to serve the purpose for which it was created, a Paradise, a Heaven on Earth.

"The greatest fear is ignorance.

The greatest gift is the release from fear.

Wisdom is that gift.

Reject and remain fearfully ignorant.

Accept and become truly free."

'Spirit'

INTRODUCTION.

We are given to understand by geologists that the earth three hundred million years ago was one land mass and one water mass. It is my understanding through the creation myth in Genesis that this earth provided a world that was perfect. An afterthought appears to be the creation of humankind. However, whereas the story in Genesis gives definitive stages for this creation, I understand that the process of creation was gradual and beginning at some far off, infinite past. Of course, this understanding does not comfort the scientific mind that constantly seeks to prove or disprove the hypothesis. Spiritual understanding is based on acceptance of what is and the trust of all that preceded the 'now' was part of the Divine order and the creator of 'now', as 'now' is the creator of the future. we are also given to understand that creation is by the hand of God and does not include the creation of God. God is the essential ingredient of all that is in this universe.

This land mass that was part of the earth, and the sea mass, were composed of all the essential ingredients that would support and nourish all future life. We also know that three hundred million years is only the recent past as far as the life of this planet is concerned, and the emergence of human form is more recent still. The Divine essence of God permeated all of creation, and still does. The Divine essence can be divided into four elements, the elements of earth, air, fire, and water. it must be considered in this hypothesis that we are not treating these elements as material substances, no more than we would see masculine or feminine energies in any physical sense either. We are talking about energy, and specifically Divine Energy. This energy is barely tangible to the now coarser sensitivity of the human but seems quite tangible to most other animals and indeed plants. The landmass contained these four elements in harmony and perhaps this is why we call it paradise. When the land mass started to break up the elements divided and separated, and eventually became as we see it today.

Many years ago, I was introduced to the philosophy of the indigenous people of the land known as America to the white people, but to the native people, it is known as Turtle Island. They call themselves "People of the Earth". Taking Earth in this title into a Spiritual context and seeing it a part of Divine energy it takes on a very different significance and poses questions about the other three elements and what indigenous races represent them, and what is their spiritual significance. Meditating on this question I was given to understand that the other elements are represented by the indigenous Spirituality of Ireland, India and Australia. The Irish are subject to and representative of the element AIR, The Indian to the element Water, and the Aboriginal to the element FIRE. If one is to theoretically apply this to these races, to their creation stories, to their culture we can see that there are persuasive signals that this is so.

The Irish creation story is that we came from "the AIR and the High Air". Many see this suggesting that we came from the stars or some constellation, however, I see this as suggesting that we came from 'higher' still, from God. The Native American talks of the emergence, but also look to the stars. The Native Indian recognises its Sacred Rivers, and the Native Australian, who refer to their country as The Land, believe that they were dreamed into existence, and are the masters of fire.

It is my opinion that all elements are unique and equal and interdependent on each other. However, only the element of AIR is beneficial to the three other elements. Any of the other elements can destroy the others, including AIR. On the negative side, water quenches the fire, turns the earth into mud, and soaks the air. On the positive side, water can be used to dampen down the fire that has gone out of control, nurture through the earth and freshen the air. If one is to think that all these features are within the ranges of our senses to experience and are but an example if the Divine nature of everything, yet we give them very little thought, we fail to recognise the eternal presence of God, we fail to recognise the Spiritual significance of all life and its interdependence. The element of Air was the first to be defiled. In our Ancient history, this country was invaded by external forces, our people subjugated, our customs altered and abused. Later history shows how our sacred, indigenous ways were destroyed and replaced, first by the Celts and then by the Christians. The spiritual element of AIR became polluted. A similar fate befell the spiritual element of WATER, India with the invaders entering the Indus valley, again imposing their ways rather than adopting the indigenous ways. more recently the spiritual element of EARTH was occupied by European people and the representatives of the element EARTH were overthrown, and this is still ongoing. Even more recently we see that the spiritual element of FIRE has suffered the same fate as EARTH and also see that this is still ongoing.

The people of the AIR, and the people of the WATER need those people of EARTH and FIRE to remind us of our spiritual nature and ways so we can restore GOD into our cultures and lives. Unfortunately, both EARTH and FIRE are slowly dying at the hands of the usurpers. I feel now is the time for these four elements to be reunited and together return this Earth to being the paradise it was created to be. Let our Spiritual Powers combine.

Maybe it is no coincidence that I live close to the banks of the sacred Shannon river, a river that 'divides' the Republic of Ireland?

CONTENTS.

Separation.

CONTENTS contd.

Reunification.

CONTENTS contd.

SEPARATION.

SEPARATION.....

1.

At this point my Spirit communicators took over the control of the writing. They wrote.......

"Over the millennia and after the divisions of the land mass it could be said that what appeared to be the deconstruction of creation began. However, there is another hypothesis we would like to share with you. In the ancient records, whether written or verbal there is constant mention of God and also the mention of an opposer of some form be it called the devil or evil. If in the beginning there was only God then where did this opposer come from? Could it be that this also was part of the creation, that God created what is called evil? God created the Law of Cause and Effect. The effect could be right or wrong, good or bad. For this law to work and develop its application had to have an outcome that would show the outcome to be good or bad. How else does one know when they have made the right choice? We have spoken elsewhere about this Law being the law of Creation and how that the continued application presents continuous creation. When one applies it on an individual basis, when one applies it to their life, one gets an insight into one's own life and how appropriate it is. If this is done then there is the opportunity to see how creative or destructive your life is. There is no case where it is neither. Do you not consider a waste of time to be destructive? Human lifetime can be measured and is limited. If one is not using it creatively then they are using it to waste. When you realise that there are no excuses nor any right to blame then you bring it all upon yourself and see then the change that needs to occur in your life to give you the creative outcome that you came to this life to achieve. So you see there is no evil, there is no devil, there is only your awareness or lack of awareness, or another word ignorance.

If again we address the content of the biblical creation of humankind, we see that God placed into this paradise humankind and that all troubles started from that point on. Remembering that this is a mythical tale and that it carries a moral to it, it is valid that we try and understand what we are being told by it. We are being told that before humankind came into existence there was perfection, that God gave guidance, that the early humans went against that advice and because of the Law of Cause-and-Effect humankind to all intense and purpose created negativity through ignoring God's advice. In a nutshell, humankind has been choosing to ignore God advise since then and that is why so much chaos persists today. God advice is always available should one seek it, and be prepared to accept what they are given. How often God hears the imploring, the requests for assistance, how often God finds the same mind closed to God's response.

So, we can see how negativity, evil, are whatever you choose to call it persists. God is the creator of all that is positive including the Law of Cause and Effect but humankind are the creators of the need for the events or situations in life that have results that do not favour the perpetrator, results that are not evil as such but are harmful or negative to the human, a product of their own creation. Over the many years of human existence, humankind has developed as a very strong force that opposes God. Humankind has created what could be called the devil. It is like the story of Adam and Eve and how they committed to original sin and destroyed paradise. Nothing has really changed since then except to have gotten worse and more "normal", where bad or negative behaviour has become acceptable and the norm. If you like this negative behaviour is the cause of further division. Human actions without reference to God are the manifestation of the separation of humankind from God."

Separation and Reunification of the Elements.

SEPARATION.....

2.

"Edmund Burke is quoted as saying, "The only thing necessary for evil to succeed is for good men to do nothing". Perhaps it should read "good humans". Do you consider yourself to be a good human? Ask yourself what have you done and what will you do for the common good? Maybe one place to start is to reintroduce the smile into our lives. Smile and feel love. Smile towards the neighbour, smile to those who look sad, smile to those who look to be in pain, but remember to smile in love. A smile does not just affect the lips but also can be seen in the eyes when accompanied with love. The love quotient is the God in your smile. Smile and love and bring back God into your life, and indeed into the lives of others.

Look into your world today and observe how much division exists. Everywhere you will see that humankind is being trained to divide in order to conquer. The children in school are being trained to compete. The children at home are being trained to compete. Sides are being drawn up in society. There is the class structure, upper middle and lower classes and subdivisions of each. Communities are being developed and classified. There are gated communities, gated to protect themselves from other communities. There are Urban and Suburban communities. There are villages, towns and cities. There are counties, or shires. There are provinces and states. All are dividing and dehumanising. Further divisions are caused by religions and beliefs, none having room for the other. Where is there space for cooperation? Where is there a facility of complementarities? Where is there an opportunity for all to come together?

Unfortunately, history has shown us that the only way that this can happen is when divisiveness becomes intolerable violence and war ensues. This appears to be the only way humanity sees as providing a solution. This is how humanity shows its spiritual ignorance. This "solution" only changes the boundaries and retains the divisions. Violence and war has never solved this problem, even after thousands of years of war, and has only lead to the further destruction of humanity. It seems that the days when neighbour helped neighbour has gone. The day when one community helped another community, when one state helped another state, when one country helped another country, when one continent helped another continent, has gone. Love without condition has gone.

Creation was and is perfect, when it is a God creation or God inspired and infused creation. When the human sees itself as being god and in competition with the God then the obvious situation occurs, negativity manifests. Look at the abundance of alternatives to nature that are being offered. Most of these alternatives are poor imitations of nature and can cause serious malfunctions within the lives of humanity, and even with the lives

20

of so many other aspects of life on Earth. Why is there a need for the chemical substitutes when there is the natural product? Humankind believes the world is expanding, what a folly this is.

Look to Ireland as an example, a country of eight million people prior to the famine and can now barely support a population of four and a half million. What does this suggest? It used to be when a couple married the community would get together and build them a house. These days the authorities wouldn't give planning permission unless certain criteria were met. Is it not strange that these criteria suddenly become relevant when for thousands of years the old way functioned perfectly, where cooperation was the solution? There is so much waste in society these days. Everything in nature complements something else and there is no waste. The same can be said of spirituality, the understanding that humanity can complement all other aspects of nature and working with nature waste nothing. One cannot live spiritually any other way. One cannot truly live without recognising the God aspects of themselves and of others, and of all things. There is no life without God."

Separation and Reunification of the Elements.

SEPARATION.....

3.

"The God of religion has always caused division, whereas true God is a unifying God. To see God as the Creator suggests that we are all descended from the One and therefore all are related. Of course, this hypothesis relates to a spiritual union, a spiritual relationship. This would also suggest that spiritually, we are all related to each other and to everything created by God. Creation was not haphazard. Each and every part of creation is a unique form, nothing is identical though could be considered similar. Each Spirit is unique and created to serve a very certain purpose.

Humankind gets confused between the physical being and the Spirit being. They get confused between the purposes that each is in the Earth world for. Many think that life is measured by physical or material success and few realise the true purpose of their incarnation. It is often wrongly assumed that life on Earth is about being born without an agenda and perhaps as a surprise for those who were responsible for providing the means of the physical body, and then to die at the other end of the lifespan. The bit between the birth and death is filled with surviving as long as one can. This is not the case. Every moment of that particular span of life, the incarnate existence, has great significance to the incumbent Spirit. We have said how earth life is a part of continuous creation. Every thought, every step taken, every decision made is the "cause" that creates the detail of the next moment, the "effect". Many think that life is unfolding but in the "effect" it is creating. There is a destination to be achieved.

This destination is more like a temporary stopping point where one rests before the next stage of creation. If you consider the preparations made before a vacation and see that before you, your Spirit came to earth, you also prepared. In the preparation you would have worked out an itinerary, you would have set out certain goals to be achieved and of course you would have chosen a suitable mode of transport, your body, to enable you to have a fulfilling holiday. Life's journey could also be like a holiday except you left your itinerary behind you. If only you could remember what your plans were. But then realising you are "lost" you accept any assistance offered.

Unfortunately, the assistance you are seeking will come at a cost, you can become dependent. Your life is now out of your control and will not be handed back to you that easily. At some stage you will take control back, even if it is to choose to die. The fact you are alive means someone is in control of your life though not necessarily you. Ask yourself what are your dependencies? If you have any outside of yourself then these are the controllers. Your needs are the welcome controllers as these are the motivators. Wants on the other hand are the unwelcome controllers in your life. The latter are the drivers and not the motivators. In another publication we say that, "Wants are for the body, needs are for the Spirit". Wants tend to divide, needs bring together. And then there is greed. Greed causes division also, and more so. Look to aboriginal cultures. Wherever in the world they are, even if they are oblivious to the existence of others, they are fundamentally all the same.

All indigenous cultures are self-sufficient, living off the bounty of Creation. The closer they are to the centre of the Element they are "powered" by, EARTH, AIR, FIRE, and WATER, the closer they are to their nature and the ideal life for them. They work as a team with interdependency. Each member has particular skills, all are sharing their abilities and also sharing the proceeds gained by employing their uniqueness. All indigenous cultures recognise the existence of God. Life is all about being, being who you are, being with your chosen body, being in tune with its necessities and of course aware of your own needs. Pursue those needs and the rest will rest will follow. The more you practice this the happier you will be, a contented Spirit."

Separation and Reunification of the Elements.

SEPARATION.....

4.

"The sign of the true artist is the degree of their own energy that they put into their work. There are many who consider themselves artistic but in reality, they are only copyists. Even landscapes artists are mostly copying that which was created by God. Photographers too merely record that which exists and are not in general creative artists. A good artist will endeavour to capture a moment in the process of creation, recording the marvel of God's work. As we have stated elsewhere creation is continuous. It is often considered that the act of creation was a past event. Any changes since that event have been attributed to humankind. Humankind is a product of creation and like all is continuing to takes its part in that process. When one realises their Divine importance and can put their ego in its proper place the human input into the creative process becomes God-driven. The Spirit can evolve and the life the body experiences is fulfilling. When this awareness is incumbent in the being the true artist manifests. The human spiritual vision adds the 'colour' to life's canvas. It enhances rather than replaces.

All that was needed to sustain the world as created by God was provided and is still being provided through nature. Unfortunately, humankind is impatient, untrusting, irresponsible and reactive. When life goes smoothly and without stress the human becomes complacent. With complacency comes inactivity and the stalling of 'time'. Time as you know it to be, measured in hours, days and years, is not as we know it. Again, we go back to continuous creation where everything takes its place on the 'timescale' of cause and effect. Active participation in life involves causing certain events to happen and the resolution of the effect caused. If the event goes well there is a tendency to sit back and enjoy the outcome. In the meantime, life continues on. When the recalcitrant realises that life has passed them by, they become anxious about what they have missed. In the panic to catch up the tendency is to look for shortcuts rather than address the situation through Spiritual awareness. The ego nature takes over and the path of perceived least resistance is sought and taken. This is the path to perdition, the gateway to 'hell'. In most such situations the conditions can deteriorate to the stage where the pursuant arrives at a point where the multitude of options are reduced to two, do or die.

It is a strange phenomenon that this is the point where most egos are shed and Spirit has the opportunity of manifesting. The human questions its existence. When they get past the blaming and excusing stages and passed the 'poor me' point they are so exhausted mentally and physically that they are devoid of that which has hidden their true being. They are ego-less and in the void of despair and hopelessness. They are now spiritually open to inspiration. Unfortunately, their vulnerability and ignorance of Spirit permits them to be subjected to influence rather than inspiration. Influence comes from that consciousness we term soul and can be helpful or destructive. It can also depend on and the relationship one has with their ancestors. Some might seek the influence of alcohol or other such apparently numbing or illusory substance. Some might seek solace in illness. Some might indulge themselves in self-righteous religion. Then others might be fortunate and resort to True God. God is always there and when called upon will always respond. Through God's response, the incarnate Spirit will come to the fore and relief can occur.

The mental and physical journey that ensues will take its time in direct proportion to the actions of the recovering being. The rate of recovery is always incremental. At what stage the correct path is regained will depend on the spiritual awareness being gained and the rate at which the ego is relegated to its correct position. You will see by this last statement that it is important the ego is retained but in a balanced state. On the principle that there is no going back, you are getting older by the day not younger; the recovery will set a course to intersect with your path where appropriate. This will not be at the point at which you left it but at a point where all the positive aspects of your prodigious journey are assimilated into your awareness. In God time there is never any waste."

Separation and Reunification of the Elements.

SEPARATION.....

5.

"The last statement is so true, "There is never any waste in God time". When one lives in God consciousness they are living on purpose. Simple words, but true words. Everything has a purpose; its usefulness and purpose is achieved by how it is utilised and this includes the physical being. When ego takes over and becomes the 'driver' of the body the living the body experiences is not on purpose, in other words, the living is not as it was intended. One must remember that the primary intention of the existence of the being is to serve the purpose of the incumbent Spirit. The ego is developed post birth and though part of the trinity of body, mind and Spirit, does not possess the necessary energy to survive on its own. With the ego in the driving seat, life becomes spiritually pointless. It is the supreme optimism of the Spirit that maintains life. Even then time is never wasted. The Spirit lives in God time and can never waste it.

As we have said, God time is set by the Law of Cause and Effect and is applied constantly. Even when the ego is in control this law still applies. The effect of any cause is being monitored by the Spirit incarnate and therefore never wasted. No matter how badly the ego behaves the Spirit will get the positive benefit of the lesson though the body will feel any ensuing pain. It is hoped that this pain will inform the ego. This will explain the root of all pain and suffering be it physical or mental and more often it is both. There are neither coincidences nor accidents, somewhere they have been created by the ego in charge.

We have spoken before about the ego and how it is nurtured by society and the human upbringing. As it manifests in a child its transgressions are excused. That same child as an adult is well trained in making excuses for its incorrect behaviour and to not taking responsibility for its actions. There has to be some crisis point where excuses run out and where the blame will rest firmly where it belongs. Only then will the ego retire from its dominant role. If it is remembered that all the while that this conduct is being observed by the Spirit, the Spirit is learning what not to do and what to do. While the Spirit is learning it will seek to maintain the body so that it will continue to provide the experiences it is benefiting from. Should the ego also begin to learn and continue to learn then there will be happy harmony.

The purpose of these particular writings is to illustrate the consequences of division. This section has illustrated the division between the ego and the Spirit during life. We have shown how nothing is wasted once it is in God time, how the Spirit can constantly learn through the actions of the ego nature of its human being. God has granted the Spirit free will and the Spirit can relinquish that free will on to the ego. Society doesn't prepare the ego for this responsibility. Indeed, society also tries to take over control of the body and further exposes the ego to further folly. Society desensitises the ego to the potential outcome of its actions. An example of this is where society permits murder to occur as long as it is war. It allows murder to be excused as long as it is committed by a soldier. The killing of innocents through war is termed collateral damage. Society accepts this sanitisation of horrendous events, all to society's ends.

Society has become Godless due to the intervention of religion and the desensitisation of humanity to spirituality. This is a further division. Firstly, the division within the human being between the ego and the Spirit, and now we see the division between Humanity and Spirituality."

Separation and Reunification of the Elements.

SEPARATION.....

6.

"There are many in your world who proclaim to be spiritual, to provide spiritual services and who form or become part of so-called spiritual communities. We are aware that many of these are anything but spiritual. Rather they are using the term spiritual to hide their ego. If one doesn't declare their allegiance to God, recognise that part of what they are, and all they do is done in the name of God, then they are not entitled to think of themselves being spiritual, let alone call themselves spiritual. We understand that there are very many spiritual human beings who because of their upbringing can have been misguided into believing their religious beliefs or denomination signifies their God connection. This is not so. They are extremely well intentioned but their belief is standing in the way of their truth. There is a fundamental truth that all religions share and that is as close to spirituality as they come. This truth is the spiritual truth but only a small aspect of the truth. Perhaps it is sufficient to fool those followers of those faiths into thinking theirs is the only way.

Ask yourself this question, if all religions share the same fundamental truth why are they so different and in conflict with each other? If they were truly spiritual, they would all be the same, there would only be one religion. We again remind you that this is the divide and conquer process that is a manifestation of negativity, a manifestation of human ego.

God is in everything and everywhere, omnipresent and omnipotent. God is always to be seen if one is but to look around them. Your eyes have been desensitised by the development of your ego. Your hearing too has been desensitised and can no longer hear God amongst all the incessant noise in your world. God's words get lost amongst the idle chatter of vacuous conversations. The vision of God is lost in the dressage of frivolous fashion. The sense of God lost in the many translations of inspired words. Can you not see? Can you not hear? Can you not sense the truth that is God? A spiritual being could. A spiritual being has many abilities that are no longer within the remit of the ego-imposed mind. The ego can only serve itself, can only hear itself, and can only see itself.

With practice this can all change. Firstly, one needs to become aware. You might ask aware of what? That question is the first obstacle one needs to overcome. Many will wait to hear an answer but only with human ears. Any answer will be missed and the questioner will satisfy themselves with an assumption. In order to provide awareness, one must first be inspired with a hypothesis. This provides the platform on which God can present the answer. The hypothesis in this instance is that there is an answer but that answer will come from life. Life is the tableau in which the human being with God jointly illustrates meaning. God paints the beauty; humankind paints its awareness. If one is to look at the life as they portray it they will see whether God is in it or not. Of course, God has participated but the lack of awareness doesn't allow the other artist to see what God has done. If one is to ponder the image with the understanding that God is in there somewhere then that small hypothesis allows the beginning of awareness. In time the God in life will emerge into full visibility. The extension of this awareness will allow for God to be seen in everything everywhere and without any doubt."

Separation and Reunification of the Elements.

SEPARATION.....

7.

"Before passing judgement on anything, or anybody, always put foremost in your mind that Creation is perfect. With this thought in mind, you might find yourself less inclined to judge. In nature, and this includes human nature, everything thing is perfect and necessary and therefore has a place. You might find this strange and be in a position to provide a list of what is wrong or imperfect or unnecessary in your life, but then have you really thought this through and without the hypotheses we have provided? Many barely listen to the question before they have an answer. Many answer without thinking. Even that which you, having thought about it and still see as unnecessary, imperfect, and perhaps even classify as evil, when connected back to God becomes again part of the perfection.

The real difficulty is the human reluctance to accept what they are presented with and to deal with it in an appropriate manner. Because of this, your world has descended into chaos.

Many race to resolve difficulties that are not theirs to resolve. Many hurry to classify their difficulties as negative as it is inconvenient for them. Much of what was presented as a problem has been because of the God-less creation of humankind. These creations stem from the concept that creation can be flawed. This is not so. There really is only one creation and though it is an ongoing process it is none the less perfect. One could say perfection becoming more perfect. It is when the closed mind of humanity seeks to outwit the Law of Cause and Effect that any hint of imperfection can exist. And even then, it is perfect. It is perfect that the human challenges the Law as then they will have the perfect lesson of, "What you sow, so shall you reap". By challenging the Law, they will get the answer, whether they like it or not, and it will always be the perfect answer.

Look around you, what do you see that you consider imperfect. Some see the human form as a frail structure in which to house such a powerful being as a Spirit. Some see a weak and twisted body in need of special care and attention as a crime against the person, as a punishment, as a liability, perhaps even of not being entitled to be born. Some look askance at the frail sick bodies of others as imperfection. Terms such as euthanasia and abortion are presented as suggested perfect solutions to these "problems". Spirit would like to draw your attention as to how these "crippled" beings came about. Let us again hypothesise. Rather than blame God for being cruel to present these "difficulties" for the word to "deal" with, assume that they are with you for a good reason and are only the outcome of some cause. But then ask yourself the question as to what caused this effect and the answer is the choices made by humanity. For some unknown reason, humanity is constantly trying to perfect perfection, usually through science.

When humankind follows a certain path, something needs to occur that will confirm it is the right path to follow. It might lead one or maybe two to their proper destination but not everyone. They too have the path they need to follow in order to arrive where they need to be. This is one of the perfect dilemmas people find themselves in. It can be a happy or sad place, comfortable or painful; it's always the right place no matter how it is. It's the perfect place to be to find out if it is the perfect place for you. If it's happy then this is where you should be, if it's sad then it's not your place, and it's still the perfect place no matter what. That's where your chosen path has taken you. Of course, having arrived there you are then set with the task of letting the outcome go and striking out afresh from where you now find yourself, always a good starting point. However, this time bring God into your planning process. See the stepping stones that are being placed in your way. God knows the way and will direct you through the power that already exists within your being. God has given you the feelings of happiness and sadness to guide you on your path, as you have also been given comfort and pain. Always seek that which gives you comfort and happiness and you will always be in your right place, and always with God."

Separation and Reunification of the Elements.

SEPARATION.....

8.

"Many are the adverse influences that act upon the human being. These influences manifest through the ego of the susceptible individual. An unenlightened mind is the fertile ground on which these influences feed. How can one expect to deliver clean water through dirty pipes? How can one expect to deliver spirituality through a contaminated channel? You will have heard of trust.

Unfortunately, the illicit use of this word has made its use untrustworthy. There are so many words that have been depowered by misuse that their true meaning no longer applies. Spirit has a mastery of words in any language but finds that it is getting increasingly difficult to make spiritual sense using the vocabulary and vernacular of modern language, Slang has become the norm. Drug fuelled parlance has been adopted, and implanted as standard speech. Language has been used to control the masses and, in some places, the native tongue has been all but eradicated and replaced with the language of subservience. It is through this "new" language that influence and control is exercised and division implemented.

If one is to consider what they are trying to say and what they actually say we think you will begin to understand what it is we are saying. You will realise how difficult it is for you to truly express yourself, to express your true self. Frustration ensues and then submission and then agreement, all the time stealing your power. As an example, ask yourself why would you need an intermediary to speak for you in a court of law, in an interview with your bank manager? What is it that these when acting on your behalf can say that you cannot? They have the language on their profession, a very different language to the layman even though the same words are used they are used in a different and more powerful manner. When one has this awareness then they can embrace the full power of what they say and further empower their word with the illustration of their actions. Those who train animals will understand this. Watch how the same command given to the same animal by two different people effects the actions of the animal. It is the power behind the words of the commander.

Influences can take effect through the use of speech and action. The ability for the recipient of these verbal influences to understand them and thus make decisions around them would depend on the degree of awareness that this recipient has on the subject in question. Can you read a legal document like you can read a novel? Can you read a music score like a book of words? The music score is also a book though it is employing a medium a musician can understand. Most music is inspired whether by the ego or the Spirit of its composer. These words are being inspired by me through the medium of my transcriber. Through these words we are seeking to influence your thinking, to enable your latent awareness to return into its spiritual ability to discern the truth, not only in what we say but the truth of the many influences. One cannot be expected to use their spiritual nature to adjudicate on their influences unless their spirituality is dominant in their life.

Because humankind has been re-educated to suit the needs of human society's controllers and their being spirituality desensitised through the influence of religion or no religion, it is well-nigh impossible for the average person to have a successful incarnational experience without falling into the many traps that negativity sets for them and by being foiled by their own ignorance. It is the individual that suffers for their own lack of awareness and the negativity that gain. Blind belief, blind faith, blind trust, are the ways instilled on the human being. God has been largely replaced by 'Mammon', truth has been replaced by belief and trust has ceased to be known as it has been replaced faith. The human ego has become the dominant force in your world and Spirit has become confused with the soul, the body and the mind. Your trust in God will be tested but you won't realise you are being tested until you appear to fail. That failure will indeed be your success as it will open you up to your God-ness. Better still you test yourself as you will be a better student to your inspired teachings, and these teachings will be administered in a less "harsh" way than by the immutable Law of Cause and Effect. Go with God."

Separation and Reunification of the Elements.

SEPARATION.....
9.

"We would at this point like to clarify some details. Many when they think of Spirit think of God, think of guardian angels (Spirit Guides), think in the terms of physical forms. When you are told you are in God's image this does not imply God has human form. This is a spiritual reference and refers to your God-likeness, your Spirit-likeness, indeed the Spirit that you are even while wearing human "cloths". Remember everything in creation has the essence of its creator imbued within its existence.

If it is your wish that you put a form to God, Spirit, your Spirit, the Spirit of another, then perhaps you will see it as the brightness of the Sun, the shimmer in the air around you, the feelings of peace, joy, and love. These would be better and closer images. Better still is to develop the knowing that all these are constantly present with you and connected to who you are, a Spirit incarnate.

Should you decide then to persist in dressing Spirit in human garb, a physical form then you may as well throw a sheet over the energy and call it Casper, at least you see that Spectre as friendly. Of course, we jest at your expense but that is only because you show us, we can. To those who like to place a physical male or female torso with large wings and discreetly placed fabrics around their concept of what they see represents an angel we say "what you see is what you get". In other words, you do not get the Divine Messenger you think you have evoked but more likely some Spirit that is still wrapped in its ego and at best a Spirit that has to return into the ego form you have created in your mind before it can communicate with you. More often you will have conjured a soul rather like the Genie in the bottle that you seek to control and to fulfil your "desires". There are many fables that illustrate the folly of such practices. Humankind has been duped into believing that these fables are mere entertaining stories whereas they are very often inspired tales carrying a strong moral guidance.

It is within the ego nature of humankind to see everything as having physical substance and dressing it accordingly. It is within the spiritual nature of humankind to recognise the presence of the creator within everything that may be called natural. Take for example the innocent weed known as a Dandelion. Many see these as being toxic to the beauty of their garden. This plant pre-existed any of the plants that you placed in your garden. It was created by God for a purpose and possess a Spirit to give the plant its life force and is there on purpose. Because it doesn't suit your requirements, doesn't fit into your design you pull it, cut it, poison it and even burn it. One might suggest that your ignorance of the Divine nature of all of creation inhibits your being able to grasp the importance of such a prolific plant. It could be that this one plant could be your saviour. When next you visit your garden look at it with your spiritual vision, see the presence of God in all you survey. Find out how clever Creation is by how it provides the treatment for every ill that the human can experience. Look how other creatures know how to use nature when they need to. From the moment it is born the honey bee seeks the flower. The Dandelion we referred to earlier is much sought after by all insect life. It could also be sought after by humankind also, if the human could only inform itself to its benefits. Ancient knowledge has an application even in modern times. All 'natural illnesses' have a natural cure. It is the sickness generated by the toxic human mind that presents the difficulty for cures. It is indicative of the industry that has been created that generates profit from a sickness that has been created by the mental and physical pollution caused by humankind, an illness created by the dominance of the ego of the human and an illness created by the absence of the human understanding of its place in creation, and of its Divinity.

It is always within our remit to wait for the call from the Spirit of humankind and to offer guidance where it is sought. In order for the human Spirit to connect with us it is first necessary that the ego provide a 'doorway' for the call to escape from its confines. This doorway is called awareness. Very often it is created by the inspired question but even more often by calamitous events in the human's life. Our response is instantaneous. The effect of our intercession may take time to be seen, it depends on the rate of positive development in the recipient's awareness. It will always be there none the less. Please avoid giving us shape or form when calling on us as we are better disposed to assist from our spirituality rather than to don the mantle of humanity. You can even address your call to God if you have any doubt. It is always God and of God."

Separation and Reunification of the Elements.

SEPARATION.....

10.

"You will notice that we are not giving a definitive instruction on "How to be Spiritual". If we were to do so would be indicative that we are not Spirit. There is no definitive truth and we can only offer our understanding of what we have experienced as being Divine truth. A truth is a dynamic unfolding of many elements, in your life one experience has so many interpretations that it is often difficult to find what it is that your event is seeking to tell you and tell you in truth. Remember the Law of Cause and Effect. The effect is the truth of what was the cause. Let's look at this another way, if you don't accept the effect as truth you will repeat presenting your life with similar causes until you get the desired outcome. Of course, the outcome will only be another version of the truth, but a truth none the less.

Let me try to illustrate this to you. Imagine you are walking on the seashore when the tide is out. The beach you are on allows you to walk out a mile before you reach the water. When next you are on the same beach the tide is in and you only have a narrow strip of sand to walk upon. The only thing that has changed is time and in Spirit where time is measured by events, the events in this story refer to the actions of the tide. In both cases the facts were true but you were misled by your ego into thinking the observations you made were deceptive. You were sure the sea was sufficiently far from the shore to allow you miles of space on which to walk, which in the first instance was true, yet on the second instance, you had little space, which was also true though not to your liking. This is to illustrate that though the effect of any cause can be different and true it is the timing and the circumstances that determine the outcome. There are always so many factors that need to be considered before the truth can be seen. Humankind is so often reluctant to accept everything as it is and the truth that is in every outcome. Many pray for particular outcomes to events in their lives, often with the fixed notion as to what they wish that outcome to be. God always hears the prayer but cannot fulfil the expectations of the person praying since their vision of the outcome makes it impossible to service their requests. God can only ever present the truth and in this instance, this was in truth a request God could fulfil. However, if the pre-conceived vision of the outcome were not there, then the circumstances would be different, and the outcome would usually be greater than the prayer sought for.

It is this reluctance to accepting what it is that generates what is called science, chemistry and associated professions. There is an industry that seeks to prove the non-existence of God and to question the veracity of Divine creation. Why is this, is it because the ego of humankind sees itself as God? Have you noticed how science acquiesces to what it cannot prove and then seeks to synthesise it, and claim to be the inventor? Columbus was said to have discovered America whereas he only found what was already there. Pharmacists' claim to have created cures for illnesses, yet they only found what was already there. We cannot claim to possess the definitive truth any more than God can. Truth is specific to the moment and the circumstances. As there is continuous creation there is continuous creation of truth. Your past is your truth and the first step in unfolding your spirituality is for you to accept that. Then there is the need for you to accept the present as being of your creation and all the associated responsibilities that come with the truth of that. When you find and use what we are imparting to you in these writings it will assist you in assimilating your truths into your life. In this way, you begin to find your spiritual path, your spiritual purpose and manifestly become the spiritual being you truly are, a unique aspect of Divine truth, a Spirit incarnate."

Separation and Reunification of the Elements.

SEPARATION.....

11.

"One cannot but sense the excitement of the earthbound Spirits and how they are excited by the egos that entomb them. We talk of the effect of human decadence upon the spiritual journey through the earthly realms. We talk about how the potentials of Spiritual advancement through the living human can be thwarted by the figaries of the human ego.

The human mind is a two-track system with both systems running parallel, one track for the Spirit and one track for the ego. They are constantly at loggerheads often pulling in opposite directions. The Spiritual track is fixed by the predetermined path set by the Spirit prior to its choosing the body that it reincarnated through. The ego track is volatile and variable and is determined by the upbringing and conditioning of the environment in which it has found itself. The human being is merely a servant to its master and the master is the mind. It could be said that the body becomes confused by not understanding the duality of its master and which aspect to be subservient to. This is what you would know as "Lack of clarity". It is not unfortunate however that this confusion exists as it causes you to stop and reason your constant future and any decisions you need to make. Many act compulsively and spontaneously without thought or reference to which master they might be serving. An example of this is when one seeks to offer advice, especially where there is a crisis. Many speak without listening first. Many answer before the question is even asked fully. Many believe they have heard the question the way it was asked whereas they were so busy compiling an answer that they heard the question in a way they wanted to be able to answer. In these scenarios, there is no doubt the ego is the master. The advice that will be proffered will be the advice that satisfies the ego of the advisor and often contain little reference to the confusion of the one seeking the advice. It is often found that the seeker is fragile and unable to resist the advice given. A strong person who seeks advice will apply discernment before acting upon the views proffered by another. The strong person will be coming from a place of calmness whereas the fragile person will often be coming from panic.

If one is to realise who they truly are they will have an understanding of the duality of the mind. If they are to ask themselves which master they are listening to and maintain this awareness, it will change the nature of their exploration of their future potentials. It will clarify what aspect of their received advice to accept and follow. One may listen to many sources of guidance but must always follow the picture that is of their application of the diversity of opinions they have been exposed to. In the end they have to take responsibility for their actions.

In the light of this information watch your own way of living. How much of your life has been determined by you acting on the advice of others, be they your ancestors, your nurturers, your educators or your friends or a combination of all of these? Your past, when the ego is applied, will contain much focus on "bad" decisions and self-deprecation. When spirituality is in place there will be humour around your "mistakes" and acute discernment gleaned from all past experiences. There is no such thing as bad advice; there is only unfortunate blind heeding of the opinions of others and the ignorance on your part as to which master you are serving.

A spiritual life is one based on fact; an Ego life is one based on fiction. When one leaves that body behind the ego will still accompany the Spirit in the form of the soul. If you leave that world without the clarity of fact you, your ego will still disparage itself until such time as it begins to understand itself. It will then take its proper place and relinquish its hold on the Spirit and allow the Spirit to continue on to the world of Spirit consciousness, allow the Spirit to enter home."

Separation and Reunification of the Elements.

SEPARATION.....

12.

"It is a sad reflection on the intelligence of humankind when they measure spirituality against religious performance. Religion and spirituality are diametrically different. Religion is practiced by the ego and is not necessarily a spiritual practice. The religion that recognises the aspects of God as a trinity is ill informed. The trinity is limiting the concept of God as it only allows three aspects to what is multifaceted. The idea that the concept of the trinity presents is a creation of humankind, and like the life concepts that are socially acceptable, are restricting the development and progression of the Divine plan of creation.

If one is to look around themselves, they will see a myriad of substances that hold an aspect of God within them. There are numerous 'trinities', earth fire and water, body mind and Spirit, hook line and sinker, he she and it. The one that misleads is father son and Holy Ghost. God is the common title for The Spirit who is a multifaceted being by composition. You, the Spirit incarnate, are a facet of God. When aware of who you are everything you touch, see, feel, hear, scent, becomes a part of the multifaceted Divine nature of God through you. Such is the responsibility of being you. No religion gives you that power and responsibility, rather is removes that from you. Your allegiance to The Spirit has been reassigned to the God of the religion you have been initiated into when you were at a vulnerable age post birth. Before you reject what it is we are saying, remember all is by your choice, even this reassignment.

No blame must be placed at the feet of another. You might seek to blame your ancestors but you chose them for the 'launch pad' into this life you have also chosen. You might now ask yourself why this is so? It is so then you might question your life and only find the answers through living it. Physical life is for the Spirit incarnate not for the body. We find that religion suggests otherwise. Religions suggests you are born in sin, that you are imperfect, that you are in that world to make amends for past transgression, often referencing past lives. There is no punishment for your past especially when you the ego realises the wonderful spiritual opportunities this life is affording you. Many accept the misconception that a tough life, a life of suffering is the way to succeed. Many enjoy the excuse that there "is no gain without pain".

Would you believe us if we said that your past has made this life easier for you, and not more difficult? You probably wouldn't but this is a fact. Everything in your life is to gladden your Spirit and to give you joy. You are capable of spreading this happiness and love wherever you go through your Divinity, through your Spirit, but only if you are in a spiritually conscious state. If you find this state difficult to access or maintain, you will find your life reflecting this in your unhappiness and discontent. Spirituality expresses God-likeness, religiosity expresses egotism.

You might find that we are against religion, we are not. You might think we are against evil; we are not. You might expect that we are fighting the ego, we are not. Why would we as they are necessary so that you can find truth by realising how these facets of human creation cause so much distress for you and how the solace of spiritual awareness returns you to your Godlikeness. All the discomforts and difficulties you experience are but the effects of what you have caused through the choices you have made, choices that are an anathema to your Spirit but pleasing to your ego. Put your Godliness first and you will never go wrong. God bless you."

Separation and Reunification of the Elements.

SEPARATION.....
13.

"The history of humankind is strewn with the interference of the human ego. In the beginning there was no ego. The celebration of everyday was common and the appreciation of the past was ever present. We have told you before of the paradise that existed at those times and how this paradise was disrupted by the advent of "shortcuts".

What we haven't really explained to you is how this all came about. Originally humankind was attuned with its nature. This attunement can still be seen in many other animals, birds, fish, and even in the insect world. This degradation in human consciousness could be considered to be a mental virus though it attacked the psychic mind and through psychic abilities. It was the advent of the ego. Its symptoms were firstly impatience, secondly greed, then possessiveness, and then anger. Many spiritual virtues became human 'sins'. Many facts became the subject of conflict where truth became a tool for deceit by being manipulated into a lie and the lie becoming the truth. Discussion, conversation, was turned into debate and egos fanned the embers of anger into the flames of war. Man turned upon man. Control of life and death became a weapon. Strife was rife. We see this as a progression into chaos and also the beginnings of the evil you experience today.

Nothing has changed for the better mainly because the ego of humankind will not face this discussion. Instead, substitutes are put in place and you are told the world is a better place for them. You are coerced into accepting the dictates of the 'powerful'. Without question you obey. Those who question are ridiculed and silenced. Nature is lost, what is left is dying. Instead of a paradise you now have a 'hell'. Such is the illusion that has been created over the millennia. This might seem like a dark and gloomy view on the life of humanity. If you look at it that way, then accept that that is how you are permitting it to be. This is how the ego would see it. If, however, you choose to look at it spiritually you will see in an entirely different way.

You are aware that things only need to get as bad in order to provoke change. If you look at the gloomy perspective your ego will see to make it gloomier and prompt you into reaction. If, on the other hand, you see the opportunity to change through your spiritual consciousness Spirit will inspire you into action. Reaction produces further reaction whereas action produces positive results. Ego will only know how to compound the issues and Spirit will resolve them. This degradation of human consciousness will change and return to normal. God will never let humankind destroy Divine creation. God will let mans creation destroy itself. We again remind you of the Law of Cause and Effect and how it is the process of continuous creation. It is constantly being applied to all forms and will let the consequences of any action show its worthiness by its continued existence and its lack of merit by its demise.

There is very little in the present state of human living that has a future. Humankind is continually moving away from its nature and from all of nature. Human dependency on the 'shortcuts' that are being still applied to living are leading humankind to its own destruction. Nothing created by humankind can survive into the future and it is not built to do so. Most of human creation is short lived and 'quick fix', whereas nature is created to last an eternity. It is important for humankind to revert to nature in order to ensure its own future. It is still not too late. There is a difficulty that we see. The human memory contains very little of what was. What was closer to what came first and to be able to follow natural progression with an open mind will enable humankind to see the wisdom and folly of past actions and reactions, even if it only pertains to one's own life. If there are any doubts look to nature for advice. Nature is still true to God, why not then the human return to its nature, return to God and thus restore paradise."

Separation and Reunification of the Elements.

SEPARATION.....

14.

"God in creation individualised the components that compose the being that has the name God. You may call it as you will as long as you realise that you are one of the components. Even as that component of God you are not exonerated from the Law of Cause and Effect. In this way you become a part of continuous creation.

This carries with it the responsibility of enlightening your own ignorance and creating your own future not only in that temporal world but also in the eternal world of Spirit. What many fail to realise true enlightenment is developing an awareness of what you don't know and the experience that educates you into that knowing, and then the realisation that even then there is so much you still need to know. This is your future, the exciting adventure of not only this lifetime in your present body but the adventure of all your past experiences in the world of matter and all the experiences to come in future lives in that world. This is an eternal quest.

You might like to think this will be your last incarnation, and many will seek to reassure you that it is. When you return to Spirit, having transited the physical and soul worlds, you will see things very differently. To your Spirit that life's journey will become worthwhile and spiritually beneficial and your Spirit will be enthusiastic for the next opportunity to reincarnate, but only when the time is right. This time will be God time, Spirit time, and will come as part of a natural sequence, a natural progression.

The time between your mortal demise and reincarnation will also be very busy. When you leave that consciousness and enter soul consciousness you will bring with you the connectors to those you loved while in that world. These connectors will be of an emotional nature. Emotions transits with you through your soul and the connectors can also be negative, or spiritually toxic. We have explained elsewhere what the soul is and how it protects the Spirit from this toxicity. We have told you how the soul also has a function and a lifetime. Until that lifetime expires your Spirit cannot re-enter this world. There is also the case that it might not wish to re-enter the world of Spirit until it is joined by those it has loved on Earth, joined it in the world of soul. It must be remembered that the soul it tainted with the toxicity of experiences that it still feels were unnecessary or negative. Not only do you carry the positive benefits of your earth experiences into the soul world, you also carry your negative and unresolved experiences with you. This is why we say that negativity and positivity exist in the world of matter and also exist in the world of soul.

Again, we would like to stress that there are no evil or negative Spirits and also stress that there are some very negative souls. These latter are commonly mistaken as Spirits by the ill-informed and can often present themselves as your 'Spirit guide', your 'guardian angel' or even a past relative or ancestor. Your discernment is so important as these ignorant souls can be so deceptive and present plausible evidence of who they are impersonating. This is the level that psychism achieves; it is only spiritual awareness that can take you to a higher consciousness that will take you out of the reaches of such negativity.

Let us focus on those loving souls who seek to help you. Earlier in these communications we illustrated how loved ones will come into your consciousness and seek to help you through inspiration and circumstance. We explained where we come from and why we refer to ourselves as we and not I. At this moment the transcriber of these words is also included in the 'we', as through his awareness we can communicate directly to your world without the encumbrance of a soul. The link we have is pure and unadulterated.

You will find that these communications might not directly apply to you but none the less the content is always informative. Who knows where these writing go and how they are carried through the awareness they generate within you, eventually a portion if not all becoming adapted and adopted into your truth? This channel is unique but not the only unique channel. We in Spirit use every available channel in any way it can be used. The purity and clarity of the channel depends on the experiences and positive awareness the medium has assimilated. These experiences include the experiences of the many past lives as well as this one. The value and operation of the channel can only be assessed by Spirit and never by anything less. There are no 'qualifications' in your world that can quantify that channel, that can endorse its veracity. The channel can only be assessed by the output and the effect it can have on one's spiritual awareness.

When you experience this spiritual benefit you will know it, it will become part of your truth and never require endorsement no matter how many might seek to suggest otherwise. Your Spirit will feel fulfilled, even though your ego might register dissatisfaction. Your trust in Spirit will never be betrayed, that betrayal can only ever happen to your ego. Many on returning to this world of Spirit will seek to return immediately to your world in the form of reincarnation. They will always have the awareness of a particular need or purpose. Sometimes this might be their need or a perceived need of others. The former will require selfishness and determination and the latter will requires sacrifice and also determination. In both cases there is always spiritual development and the creation of future opportunities.

This is a conversation for another day and will require you to have considered this communication before we can advance this further forward. It is important that you receive a clear understanding of the Law of Cause and Effect and how it distinctly applies to you and your conduct, and how all responsibility rests solely with you. You must rest and ponder these words. You cannot raise your consciousness until you relinquish the hold of the many misunderstandings you have blindly accepted as beliefs and thus lost sight of the truth that exists all around you, even though you deny it. For now, go with God's Love and understanding."

SEPARATION.....

15.

"The social and political instability in your world is creating a situation where human existence is now in a fragile state. We in Spirit see this as the result of the false gods that humankind has subjected itself to. If one is to consider how this began, one must wind back the events that have occurred as a consequence of the decision of one human being. This human was the first greedy person.

Whether it was 'Eve' seeking the 'knowledge' from the apple or seeking the 'power' it was supposed to offer, it was nonetheless the weakness of 'Adam' seeking to provide for his partner and to respond to her every whim. The 'Serpent' carries no responsibility for the ensuing events, that responsibility lays solely at the feet of 'Adam'. So, humankind left Paradise and has never sought to return. Perhaps now it the appropriate time to ask for assistance from God. Perhaps God is giving that assistance through these writings.

71

We come at God's behest, not just to this transcriber but to all humankind all the time. The difference here is that this is someone who will listen. This one welcomes the day when these communications are no longer necessary, as then humankind will have arrived at the point where they can take informed control of their own lives. Everyone has the ability to live their lives in a spiritual manner. They have been inhibited for many generations by the pressure's society has been putting upon them. If you like Adam yielded under the same pressure from Eve and chose to compromise the future of humankind by not applying better judgement to the situation. We do not want to point fingers at either male or female personas though we refer to the image of Adam and Eve. This story is popular and popularly seen as it is and not as what it illustrates. There are no other species that this refers to, only the human being. There is seldom any of the conflict between the genders of other species as there is in the human. This is what makes the human different from other animals. There is the other complication that the human has lost sight of its purpose in that world. It sees progress as material progress and not spiritual progress. It sees power as material power, not spiritual power. The Adam and Eve story is to show the starting point of human discontent and dysfunction, the "fall of the Angels", the conflict of difference. You can see this in your world when you look at human relations, how some last a lifetime and some are come crashing down.

That is far removed from anybody's idea of Paradise. You may ask how things can change. The first goal must be to achieve self-honesty. Examine how you feel about what has been just written. If you see yourself primarily as male or female you will no doubt go into a defence mode. If however, you see yourself from a spiritual perspective you will have no apparent response but will ponder these words. If you look at it from the point of view of the humankind of this time you will look to see who the perpetrator was and who the victim was and maybe even blame the poor snake for causing it. Now, look at it removing the 'luxury' of deflecting any responsibility away from you, your gender, your education or even your beliefs. Take on the role of Adam. Take on the responsibility of his decision. How does that feel to you? You have the fortunate use of hindsight to adjust your thinking. You need to realise that you unknowingly face his dilemma every day and are subject to the same responsibilities and consequences. Now you can see where you are and the opportunity for you to invoke change. If one human's choice can be the cause of the effect you are still experiencing, think then how the choice of one human now can change the future and lead the way to future Paradise.

Please see that we are not here uninvited but in response to the many requests of incarnate Spirits, requesting that their bodies be returned into their control. God has blessed you with our presence."

Separation and Reunification of the Elements.

SEPARATION.....
16.

"We have spoken before of the New Age Movement, (N.A.M.). We said that the advent of the N.A.M. was a great disservice to Spirit and a poor representation of spirituality. In our understanding, it is but another religion that blocks the vision of humankind. Religion has restructured human understanding of spirituality and has reset the human concept of what is God and introduced its interpretation of what is good and evil to control humankind.

Astrologically the universe has indeed moved into a new phase, and as this age has its beginnings under the sign of Aquarius it has been called the Age of Aquarius. This title holds little significance to those who do not know or understand astrology and less significance to astrologers who don't know or understand spirituality. Everything in creation has been created for the benefit of Spirit and its further development. Everything in creation has a role to play in the existence of everything else and including itself. The interaction of these various components that make up creation and the created is reflected throughout the universe and is dependent on the location of the component in relation to all other components. You are on the planet Earth and your life is affected by the sun, moon and all the planets in the universe in some way relative to the moment you are in. If you have knowledge of astrology you would be able to calculate that effect. The fact that this age began in Aquarius will affect all those on Earth be it animal or vegetable or mineral. The significance of this age is that it refers to the readjustment of world bringing it to a greater understanding of spiritual purpose. As New Ageism is but a barrier to this, as are all religions they will all have to be removed.

The N.A.M. straddles the boundary between conventional religion and spirituality in that it accepts many traditions that religion opposes and at the same time accepts many the aspects that these religions profess. N.A.M. suits all and offers a handy excuse for behaviour that is different to the devout practices of members of other religious denominations. It is, like all religions, power driven. It goes a long way in degrading what can seem to be spiritual practices. It advocates a myriad of energy healing practices obscuring the God-given facility of Spiritual Healing. It encourages the provision of alternative lifestyles that have no foundation in the true nature of creation where everything is perfectly harmonious and complementary. There can be no alternative to God and no alternative to God's creation.

All will change, institutions will collapse. Anything that opposes Spirit will fail. The barriers that obscure the truth will fall away. Humankind will return to its senses. There will be no end to life but there will be an end to the world as humankind sees it.

You will be driven back on to your path so that you may resume your journey of spiritual growth.

These words we give you today might appear harsh and frightening. They are not new words as they have been uttered many times before, but not in this context. There is nothing for you to fear as everything is in Divine order and governed by the just Law of Cause and Effect. Those who have what they consider to be spiritual awareness will have that conviction tested. If you are spiritually aware you will understand the changes that are occurring and will adjust accordingly without much effort. Openness to change and adaptability are the qualities that will make the changes seamless and easy to embrace. Dogmatism will only encourage pain and unhappiness.

It is not often that we come with this information and pose the potential of generating fear within you. If you find that you can trust in God then you will not suffer. If at this moment you do not know what to have trust in, please call on us and we will help you. Many have experienced the Love that is God manifest in their lives through the facility of Spiritual Healing. It was a relief from pain that was first experienced, all pain preceded the change. Change provided the means of getting back on track Spirit-wise. So too now, the Spiritual Healing of humankind is at hand.

We bring you boundless love to help you through these times."

Separation and Reunification of the Elements.

SEPARATION.....

17.

"You may well now ask where the light is at the end of this particular tunnel. This is not yet the time to tell you. You are not yet prepared through the assimilation of the content of these series of writings if you find it necessary to jump the gun and ask that question. Asking that question is seeking a short cut and we know where that led the human too when they started this particular round of spiritual annihilation and reaching the stage in that process that you are now at.

This is not the first time that humankind has achieved this status. On previous times when this occurred, they again took the path of "shortcuts" and "quick fix". The "magic wand" is now, as it was previously, contained in the word AWARENESS.

We have frequently used that word in this, and previous, dissertations. What we said in our opening statement could be rephrased by saying we have provided you with enough information that had you taken notice of it would have allowed you to have the awareness that would have answered your question, and then if you had that awareness you wouldn't even ask it. That is if you didn't want us to do all the work for you. Because we have this knowledge, we don't need the experience but you do. Remember when you become aware you will be in a state to receive inspiration and coupled with your intuition you will act accordingly.

We will continue with our communicating the necessary clues to how you can address your future as an individual, a race, and a species. If you are to look about you no other species is threatening the continued existence of another species other than the human species. The current human existence is threatening all other forms of life and to all intents and purposes will render planet earth lifeless. All this is in the pursuit of material gain. Humankind seems to think it appropriate to leave your world in an uninhabitable state so that future generations will have no future.

Dependency creates division and is but another word for subservience. There are the master and the slave. There can be many levels of slavery but only one master. Even the assistant master is a slave to the master. If you think about this and compare your life to the model we illustrate, we are sure you will find it discomforting. There are so many stories told of "selling your soul to the devil". Your subservience to anything in order that you can live is tantamount to the temptations that are presented to you by the masters, your dependency on them allowing you to live and providing the means to remain a slave.

The requirements for human existence are no different from any other species. There is only one dependency and even that is not as such. We have reassured you before that there is a provision in Creation for the continued existence of humankind.

Everything you need in order to live has been provided. The difficulty is that this provision has been removed from you by the imposition of the master and slave concept. A leader should never be in the role of master. A good leader will have mastery of many skills. A good leader will never exploit their position in order to gain power. Their leadership is a power in itself. Everyone has the authority to lead themselves and the power to do so but they choose through their ignorance to give that power and authority to another. This power is invested in a leader who inevitably will use this power to their own ends and corruptly. You surrender your power willingly by choosing to be subservient. You choose to be subservient due to your ignorance, an ignorance you have gained through "education" or as it is truer to call it indoctrination. You are educated into the system of social interaction called need and greed.

Your greed leaves you open to the temptation provided by the system and your needs which would naturally be catered for can now only be satisfied by the provisions the master feels fit to provide. You are now dependent on your master. Your master takes over your life and you no longer have the time nor the energy to provide for yourself other than further surrendering any time left to the service of your master. You are fooled into thinking how great you are yet you are never far from absolute poverty and death.

These are very grim facts of life and can cause the divisions we spoke of in our introduction. There is an expression, "Every man for himself", how true that is of the world humankind has created within the Paradise that God created, the hell on earth. The most amazing thing is that humankind still has the time to reverse this downward spiral by becoming more in tune with their own individual spirituality and being inspired as to how change can take place and the human species, and all species, animal vegetable and mineral can be saved. We in Spirit are awaiting the opportunity of helping you manifest God on earth once again before its too late."

SEPARATION.....

18.

"It must be remembered that it is never our intention to frighten you into a reaction through the words we use. Neither is it our intention to blame or criticise the actions of humankind. It is our intention however to draw your attention to the ego driven social system of a large portion of the human population, and the potential disastrous consequences of un-arrested greed by all adults within that sector. We seek to trigger your awareness by these words. It is a fact that God has given your individual Spirit free will. God has not given this free will to your ego. As the Spirit is a benign being in the world of matter it is comparatively easy for the enhanced ego to dominate it. This same unfettered ego has been inducted into the material world system of demand and supply through the "educational" system that belongs to that population.

From physical birth the developing child is conditioned, as were its parents, into the lifestyle that society desires it to live.

This practice has now become an unconscious process and considered the norm. It has little to do with what is natural, it is totally a contrived system of behaviour developed over time to further the interests of the minority at the cost to the majority of losing their spiritual purpose for their sojourn in embodiment. Spirit is only manifestly present in the innocent or aware human being. The newly born child exudes this innocence, it is palpable to even the most unaware and the child is vulnerable to the whims and wiles of the predatory "master class" that controls the lives of the child's parents. We see and increasing disrespect for the newly born with plans being made for their future, overruling whatever plans the incumbent Spirit might have. How few marvel as the awesomeness of this perfect being freshly arrived into the world.

As this child matures into adulthood it progressively loses awareness of its intended journey and replaces it with the ambitions of others. Instead of being assisted through it's journey by a "support system" it is controlled and conditioned to support the social system and the state. This persists until the human through illness or old age, can no longer make useful material contributions to the system. At this stage they are often seen as a burden on the state and on their families. In the familiar sense this burden is not recognised because of emotional responsibilities and the elder is accommodated and tolerated. However, in other societies this person would be acknowledged for their wisdom gained through a lifetime of experiences. They would be respected and revered for this awareness. They would be consulted and their wisdom would be to the future benefit of their community. In your present system these wise folk are "homed", often at great expense, and kept quiet.

You will notice a prevalence of mental indisposition and languidness amongst this sector of the population, a waste of a valuable resource left to while away their "twilight" years. These people have often a clear insight of the spiritual purpose of their life, when they are permitted by their egos to express it, but so often refrain from sharing this for fear of ridicule and disrespect for their cherished views.

As each generation grows further into the abyss of materialism the only hope for the future of the world and for humankind itself is being lost at a greater rate. We here are watching the demise of all human existence, an existence that is being touched by the avarice of so-called civilised people. The only possible survivors will show themselves after the demise of this ignorance and of the ignorant egos. These survivors will be from amongst those who have not lost, or will have regained, their Spirituality and therefore a sense of the journey they sought to take. These people will often be those that were considered "useless", stupid, uneducated, not worthy of social investment, and those who retained the indigenous ways of their forefathers. These are the people who will survive as they will have retained the natural human instincts, and the channel for inspiration, that will show them how to exist without the artificial support of the artificial material world.

The elderly though infirm still retain a mind that has a wealth of knowledge that can contribute to the future welfare of the human population on that planet. When the change begins to become more apparent it is these elders that one must turn to. The sense of family, community and state needs to be reinstated. Family history will need to be revisited so that the past can be reintroduced into the present in the form of valuable references for the future. All will become the domain of God, returned to its rightful owner. All the Godly tenants will inhabit rather than inhibit a world devoted to spiritual growth, and Paradise will be reinstated. This is God's plan. The only opposition to it will be the egos of humankind. Watch and see God's plan unfold. You are blessed with the opportunity to participate."

SEPARATION.....

19.

"We know that we have been challenging you with these past communications yet we make no excuse for this. We seek to provoke you. There is logic in this. If we can make you look to yourself and your understanding of life and yet challenge you by doing that it signifies that you are not truly confident in your beliefs. There is a difference between belief and truth and that is the reason why we state our truths. We don't have beliefs. Truth stands on its own. It never needs faith to carry it.

Listen to yourself stating your beliefs and ask yourself why they are only beliefs. They remain as beliefs until they become or fail to become your truth. You can believe in God, but that belief holds until you get to know God. Knowing God changes everything. Knowing God lets life become a spiritual reality. Believing in God is only a handy convenience. One cannot expect to provide any services in God's name while retaining God stuck in a belief system. Belief in God is a religious panacea. The profundity of knowing God will allow you to see the truth or falseness that surrounds you. Nobody can tell you your truth. We cannot tell you your truth. God cannot tell you your truth. Such is the uniqueness of truth, that is how personal it is.

You can share your truth with others but don't expect them to accept it. They hopefully will not. We don't expect you to accept what we say as truth. We hope that you will entertain us by listening. At the same time, we hope you will listen to our words and add them to your beliefs. Keep your beliefs dynamic so that they may help you access what is true for you and allow you to discard what is false for you. You can never be comfortable in the beliefs of another and be responsible for yourself. When you discover God in yourself you will be comfortable in yourself.

Where then is God in your life? God is everywhere. You don't see God because you don't know what you're looking for. You can see God in another before you see God in yourself. When you see God in that way look in a mirror and look for God in yourself. Often you will find a rush of various emotions when you practice this and often also an ego v Spirit conflict. False modesty takes place; your mind will accuse you of vanity, ego, self-gratification, self-indulgence and a gamut of other self-deprecating expressions. You will feel shy even though there is only you and the mirror, and of course God. This may take some time before you can still the mind and loose the ego self. You will find a stillness and a feeling of Divine love. You may even shed a tear of bliss. Then you will realise you are no longer looking at yourself but at God. As soon as you realise this you will immediately loose the vision and once again see your physical self. Now though, you will look at life differently and particularly your own life and how best to lead it. It is important that you do not take this vision and intellectualise it.

Please take it as a very personal and private revelation. If you seek to manifest it as a 'power' tool and suggest to yourself that you can exploit this new found you, and then you will have reverted to the old pre-vision you. From this point on you will constantly need to monitor your ego especially in the area of false modesty. When you take responsibility for your actions your will also take responsibility for the outcomes of those actions and the attention of others this will draw to you. Become attuned to your feelings and we will soon let you know if you should stray.

This awareness of God is a great blessing and if spiritually applied will unfold to show you your true purpose in life. Initially life on earth is for your ego to get to know and see God. With the ego thus informed you can then express the spiritual side of your incarnation. You can become a better human, a better partner, a better parent, a better employer, a better employee, a better friend, a better elder. On the completion of your life journey, you will have a better transit into the next phase of being. All this is promised once you get to know the aspect of God that is resident within your physical being. God blesses you."

Separation and Reunification of the Elements.

SEPARATION.....

20.

"The reunification of all aspects of creation including humankind re-establishing itself in its proper place is happening. Travel to other planets will not solve the problem. It will only spread the problem. You may think that humankind is in a unique position, one that it had never experienced before, but this is not the first time that this has happened, though one would hope that it may be the last. Your Earth has been ravaged by natural catastrophes before, each time a different calamity. All are familiar with the flood. Of course, there were survivors but the lessons were not learnt or if they were, they were forgotten.

The great tales that have lasted, and some even predate the flood, still carry the essential message from God, don't challenge Nature. If humankind were to learn from what it finds challenging then there would be a different world. A challenge only remains a challenge until it is understood and the benefits recognised. Humankind seems to think that every challenge must be met with a counter challenge but this is not the case. The only way to meet a challenge is to understand it, adopt it, and adapt it to suit you personally. Again, we find that once a person's challenge is adopted by large numbers of people, and the differing viewpoints are gathered, it now becomes a greater and unsolvable difficulty. Bedlam will now ensue. This situation could even develop into war. That's how simple this escalation is. There is one element that is seldom recognised, this has all come from the challenge experienced by one person and escalated by the interference of so many, others rushing to resolve what wasn't any of their business.

This is all to do with the non-recognition of the strong presence and dominance of human EGO. When egos run out of control God knows what will happen but because the human ego doesn't recognise God humankind won't see the signs or listen. The Law of Cause and Effect takes over. That's what will happen. That's what God knows will happen. Because of humankind's lack of awareness, they will drive themselves to their own destruction. Those who survive such conflagration will be those who learnt early enough to heed the message, and have sufficient awareness to draw all that is positive from the mayhem of ignorance that was occurring.

Nothing presented through nature or through the Law of Cause and Effect will present permanent or lasting difficulty. This is a just law. It is just a way of showing what is and isn't appropriate, It is directed to the individual response to a situation that that individual is experiencing and lets that individual know the outcome of choices they have made. When a situation is presented to one person it is for that person to resolve it. Others may offer their opinions or perspectives but no one else can resolve it for them. This is where spiritual awareness comes into play and how spiritual understandings provide the natural solutions. Take Spiritual Healing as an example. Spiritually illness is just that, as is disease, a challenge to be understood and resolved. No challenge is to be fought against. In Spiritual Healing there is no room for ego, no diagnosis, no fight back against what has naturally developed within the body of an individual and carries a message for both the body and then Spirit. The illness is being presented by the Law of Cause and Effect so that the body and mind can take cognisance of the misdirection it is taking the Spirit in. The threat of an illness being potentially terminal is only that, a threat. It is the decision of the incumbent Spirit as to whether the body should live or die. However, if the ego is dominant it will fight the illness and seek to sustain the life. This is mainly through fear of dying and loss of its apparent power.

Most medical treatment at best only provide sustenance for the body and provides extra time for the spiritual awareness to be gathered and the ego to surrender to the Spirit whilst suppressing the discomforting symptoms. Should this awareness happen then a "miracle" can take place and full health can be restored. It is sad to say so often the illness succeeds and death takes place. Though there is a death it is still the Spirits choices to withdraw from that body. If humankind can see this then there will be fewer deaths through illness though there will always be a need for death to release the soul and Spirit from the mortal coil. Conflict is a waste of valuable time. Conflict creates division. Resolution provides cohesion. Only God-likeness and God awareness can provide the tools for unity and a return to our natural Spiritual state."

Separation and Reunification of the Elements.

SEPARATION.....

21.

"There is no part or place within the creation of God that is evil. There is only one place in the universe where evil exists and that is within the creation of humankind. Only the human animal is capable of being classified as being evil. That evil is not within the Divine nature of the human but exists solely through the ego or ignorant mind of the vehicle of the incarnate. The further the awareness of the human strays from the awareness of God the greater the potential for them to encounter evil.

Because of free will God cannot interfere in the choices the incarnate makes. Positivity needs to be invited into one's life, on the other hand negativity because it resents the power of God chooses to ignore Divine rights and overrule free will. The human being who is in ignorance of its spirituality will be the easy prey for this influence. By its nature ignorance constantly seeks enlightenment. There are few sources left in your world that can provide this. Your world has become a cesspool of negativity with stagnation occurring in place of development. The progress of spiritual development has all but ceased and in its place confusion has taken over. Few invite God into their life, nor into their thinking.

We have written elsewhere of human development and how the social emphasis is on the human developing through it ego and measuring that development by material gain. There is no God in that, little good in it. Material wealth provides cold comfort outside of physical life. Those who gather such wealth at the cost of another's happiness and joy will live long enough to see what they have missed in life. Evil is within the realm of the ego. Again, we have discussed the human ego in many of our previous dissertations. Suffice to say the evil created by the human in its lifetime survives the body dying and passes into the next world or consciousness by its attachment to the soul.

The next level of existence to the earth conscious state could be called the soul conscious state. It is not yet what is called the Spirit World, the realm of God consciousness. The realm of soul consciousness contains both negative and positive energies with the potential to effect or infect one another and more to the point of this communication, to infect those in the physical world who through their lack of awareness are vulnerable to negative influence. Religion will not protect them as religion in itself has been turned fearsome. All religions empower negativity through their insistence on the threat of negativity and the suggestion that it is powerful. People are invited to fight off negativity. This implies negativity has presence and power. Religions give form to negativity by giving it a title such as evil, demon, devil, Satan. Humankind has given it form also though the many graphic representations provided by artists. Evil is merely the presence of ignorance and solely the behaviour of ignorant egos who depend on human fear to exert any influence in the human world. Religion can only go part of the way to providing any relief from this influence, as religion in itself is ignorant and relies on faith and belief to sustain itself through its followers. Spiritual awareness is the only solution to this negativity as it releases belief into truth and dispels doubt and ignorance.

If one is to embrace the hypothesis that everything is good it will bring one a long way towards awareness and the opportunity of learning more. If one is to think something is bad then they will only further empower the negativity associated with that situation or experience. It is important that one realises that "bad" is necessary in order to see what is "good". Perhaps it could be suggested that the "devil" is necessary in order to see GOD. This latter is only because humankind has become so unaware of its own Divinity. When humanity unequivocally realises that it is but an embodied Spirit the power of the human ego can become a positive power and assume its role as a support and ally for the God-likeness that is called the Human Being. With this realisation will come the natural abilities of the Spirit. The ego will have complete trust in its incumbent and negativity will have no purchase on the soul. There will be no unknown to be feared. God bless you."

Separation and Reunification of the Elements.

SEPARATION.....
22.

"It has often been said that the human world is an evil place, rather it is a place where evil exists. There is nowhere else in the universe that evil exists, nor does it exist in any other species than the human species. Humankind alone possesses that potential, and then only through its ego.

Many traits and illnesses are misjudged and misdiagnosed. Evil manifests at the hand of humankind and in many cases is an expression of the ego/Spirit conflict within the being. All illness manifests as a consequence of this conflict. If one is to apply this hypothesis there will be new treatments provided by those who take the time to follow this idea rather than look to quell the symptoms. Even so-called accidents can be averted when this philosophy is pursued.

We will remind you of the purpose of your life on earth. Your body is for the benefit of the Spirit housed within it. The journey your body takes through life has been pre-determined by your Spirit. It is designed so that you will inevitably encounter the necessary redirections should it stray from its intended path. If you like the human body is the test vehicle for the Spirit to venture into the unknown avenues of Karma. Karma is about the future not about the past, we see this fact is so often misunderstood. We have told you how Karma is the Law of Cause and Effect. We have told you that this Law is the Law of continuous creation. This law precedes any action of humankind but is only applied subsequent to any human action. Think of the chemist mixing two chemicals in an experiment that had never been tried before. The outcome is unknown though the possible outcome is predetermined by the nature of the chemicals. The chemist has hope that there will be a favourable outcome for what they are trying to achieve, but as this has never been tried before there is a certain risk involved. The outcome of the mixture is what the chemist is seeking with no knowledge as to whether it will be what is being sought or not. The experiment is neither good nor bad though the result will be appropriate. Every part of creation is a result of such 'experiments', including the creation of humankind. If one refers to the creation myth in the book of Genesis you will see that the creation of humankind was last on the list. The world of humankind is still in its experimental stage and the final outcome has not been achieved yet.

When one is delving into the unknown it is seldom blindly, there is a certain direction towards what one hopes to achieve. So too with the development of the human psyche, God has a certain plan in mind. Earth is the laboratory and humanity the 'guinea pigs'. God is the chemist and the incarnate Spirit is the element. When one element is mixed with another then the outcome is assessed and when it is thoroughly understood the goodness of the outcome will be brought further and the bad discarded. So too with your life, you need to reflect on this and see that everything in your life has a usefulness but that you need to have the discernment to adjudicate on the positive outcomes of everyday events. Incorporated in this discernment process will be your spiritual awareness and your ego. These two elements will need to be mixed correctly, Spirit first and ego second, in order to avoid any negative influence that may be present. Take as an example the conditions called illness, or sickness, or disease. How you describe your medical conditions, which of these terms you choose to use will describe the condition you are experimenting with. Whatever you are doing is making you ill, whatever you are doing is sick, or whatever you are doing is causing dis-ease. In each of these categories, it is what you are doing that is at the core. Why would anyone continue what they are doing if this is the outcome?

Many persist in wrongdoing and rely on medication to cure their malady rather than change what they are doing. Medical intervention may provide respite but only change can affect a cure. The real response to these conditions is to recognise that they are God-given through the Law of Cause and Effect and provided to enable effective change in your life, to redirect you onto your path. Your next task is to find your path and to stay on it. Many when they find wellness again through the combination of medication and change unfortunately revert to what they were doing before they got unwell. This suggests that there was a strong ego influence placing them in a situation, due to a state of mind that was unhealthy for them. It is the ego that will influence the choice to revert. It is the control of the sick society that humankind has created that will empower the ego.

In times of stress, or distress, always look to God for guidance. This is not a difficult task. The Law of Cause and Effect,

God's Law, is ever-present. Take responsibility for your actions, your choices, whatever the outcome and God will, through The Law, reward you. Go with God in Divine Love."

Separation and Reunification of the Elements.

SEPARATION.....

23.

"Negativity takes many forms and can be inadvertently invited into your life. Procrastination is perhaps the most common tool used to ruin any forward progressive spiritual growth. Any reluctance or hesitation on your part is taken as an invitation by that negative energy. Thinking negatively of any situation or person is also an invitation. Your general attitude and reactions are also worth considering. If you start your day in dread you can be sure you will have a dreadful day.

Negativity feeds on negativity. Hate gets hate as love gets love. When you react in anger to anger you will find that the anger becomes more intense and progresses towards violence. If you respond to the same anger with love and understanding the dynamics of the encounter change and the anger generally abates. Watch other animals and see how they act out such scenarios. This only works where animals have not been too domesticated. Yes, there is always submissiveness to the Alpha male or female but not subservience. The role of the Alpha leader is not one of dominance and abuse of power so often seen with the human animal; other animals are not controlled by negativity. Other animals are subject to their nature whereas the human has accepted or has been educated to be subject to other humans in the form of chieftains or political or religious leaders. All human-made laws are there to subjugate the human population and are ego based. They are 'positive' for some and 'negative' for others and seldom justice. Most human laws are negative and feed further negativity. This is the way of the modern ignorant world and the reason for so much separation.

If one is to ask themselves how this situation came about, they will find the opportunity to get an answer. All education in the world of 'modern' society is set to perpetuate this control of society by only opening the minds of humankind to the influence of negativity. Look about you and what do you see? You see unhappiness and unrest, addictions to mind controlling substances, poverty, crime, homelessness, illness, hunger, calamity, and the list is endless and very negative. This is all attributable to the type of indoctrination that human beings are subjected to from birth in the 'modern' society. If one looks then to those who have not yet been tainted by this scourge, look to untouched indigenous people. They have no judicial system, no extremes of wealth, no crime (except against natural law). They have no need dependency external to themselves. They are self-sufficient and not controlled through their ego. They live for their Spirit. Negativity has little purchase in their lives. They have no need for us in Spirit to take this action to inform humankind and to seek to dispel such ignorance that is apparent in your world these times.

May we suggest that you look at your behaviour in life and first of all ask yourself "are you happy"? If you find yourself thinking that you are there is a good chance that you are fooling yourself and being thankful for what little you might have. This is the grand illusion that has been created by your society. Do you feel you need a holiday? When on holiday do you find a reluctance to returning back into the lifestyle of home? Wouldn't it be wonderful to see every day as a holiday? Now ask yourself why is it that is cannot be so? Now say that you are truly happy. On your holiday you wake with Joy and have a joyful day.

You went into the world of humankind to experience the consequence of the actions of your forefathers and to recognise the folly associated with them. There is very little in the history of the last two millennia of humankind that is worth perpetuating or repeating. There have been many in your world that have carried the guidance towards awareness but humankind chooses to ignore their message or suppresses it totally. We will persist as we see the value of human life and its glorification of God. Humankind is "hell-bent". This is a human expression not one of ours but perhaps you need to listen to yourselves, to your own inner voice

Your world was a paradise until humankind was created and its ego took over control. Now is the time to reintroduce peace, harmony, and love. Now is the time to reintroduce God."

Separation and Reunification of the Elements.

SEPARATION.....

24.

"It is often difficult for us to communicate into the world of humankind. There is so much negativity present and invited into that world. We would remind you that we need to be invited before we can manifest our presence since we need access to the human energy field. The human energy field is that energy often called chi or life force energy. This energy is contained within the remit of the ego. The ego, when left to its own devices, will seek to enhance itself and find better nourishment from the promises made by negativity.

The ego will constantly invite negativity into itself as the ego see itself as the divine eternal being and will dress in excuses for its behaviour. The ego seldom accepts responsibility for its actions or the outcomes of those actions unless these outcomes enhance the ego. The ego only has this apparent power due to the ignorance of the human of its Spirit.

Ignorance of Spirit, and thus spirituality, occurs due to the suppression of inherent awareness and education away from God awareness. All education provided by the state or religious institutions are guilty of this and are ably assisted by the preoccupations set upon the working population to distract them from providing the spiritual welfare of the young in their care. Again, we suggest you look at the aboriginal societies for guidance on this matter. They have aboriginal "religion" which always includes God, The Great Spirit or some supreme being by whatever name. To analyse the spirituality of these diverse cultures you will see there is a commonality even though these cultures may never have met and indeed may have been separated by thousands of miles of land and ocean. If you like this could be called core spirituality. This core is the same core of all religions and needs no saviour just recognition. This core has been used as the foundation for the unchallenged structure, the society and religion of humankind. These religions are built with and by human egos, for the benefit of those egos, and are inherently negative for that reason. Yes, they provide a certain stability to society by keeping its negativity under control. When people move out from under that control you experience unrest. This unrest is due to the lack of God in these people's lives and violence erupts. There is no longer control over negativity.

A radical change in awareness is the only solution. What this form of change can offer is not attractive to the ego. It can only offer peace, love and happiness which many feel they can buy anyway, so why change? So many fail to see that even with all the riches in the world, they cannot find true happiness. Many of the so-called spiritual practices of new ageism and psychism and the many other "isms" are merely salve for the wounds caused by unhappiness. You will often hear that you must express gratitude for all you have. Yes, be grateful but to whom or what;

to be thankful for your job? to be thankful for your life? To ignore your unhappiness is to ignore God drawing you to the awareness that something is not right in your life, and that you need to change. You are told to learn to forgive, but again forgive whom or what? You are seldom shown how to understand what it is that is going on in your life, that is causing you to need "hard times" and "bad luck", and to give yourself the opportunity of changing your life into a happier and less stressful one.

Many experience periods of misfortune and bad luck in their lives but often fail to realise the turning point when life becomes easier and more comfortable. As long as they keep on giving thanks and forgiveness these periods persist. Once one realises that these discomforts are in life to tell you that you need to change and that you can do so with the help of God, the ego begins to lose its power and negativity recedes. You will find that others will come into your life to assist you and though you might be finding difficulty with making the necessary changes they will support you. Consider them a God-send.

The Love of God is unconditional and available to all. Nobody is unworthy of that love. All you need to have is an idea of God and the desire once again to be within that awareness. From that moment on you will notice improvements in the quality of your happiness and realise what you thought was happiness wasn't that at all. Life will change and become a different and easier challenge. You will never lose that understanding, though you might forget from time to time. God will always remind you."

Separation and Reunification of the Elements.

SEPARATION.....

25.

"One is never offered the opportunity for change in their lives that they do not have the ability to implement. The outcome will always be for their good. It is a matter of discernment, the awareness to encourage you to see the future will always be good when God is part of it. There is nothing in your future that you need fear, other than the possibility that you might have forgotten God.

We would again remind you that these communications are to inform you, to offer guidance, and never to command. They cannot be seen as anything but a hypothesis, an opening for you to develop an understanding of who you potentially are and what your sojourn on that planet is about. They are to remind you of what you already know but have been educated by your society to forget. They are to reinforce your spiritual resolve. They are to help your understanding of your present life and the disarray that appears to be prevalent within it. We have challenged your estimate of your happiness solely to provoke you into thinking about it. We find there is a complacency within the actions of humankind, a complacency that numbs the human senses. There is an acceptance that human life is about suffering and unworthiness.

We cannot tell you any truths for as we have already explained: "truth is personal and dynamic". There is history that is the truth but had you not lived in those times then it is somebody else's truth. No two truths are the same and this is why history appears distorted. Perhaps myths and legends are the best form of guidance that one can get from the past. They have survived the test of time. Myths and legends carry the message of the event in graphic terms and carry the essential message through to these times.

We have referred to the creation myth in these writings and the message that can be taken from it. There are other stories of creation from other cultures that are equally important but will carry the important message for that culture. Of course, the predominant culture in your world these days is what is called Western culture. This is a culture of colonisation, domination and subjugation, one stratum of society seeking to take over, rule, and control another. This is far removed from the peace, love and harmony of spirituality. This is the social sickness that is now endemic in modern society.

This is the sickness that comes from a lack of spiritual awareness. Like any sickness, there is a cure but, in this instance, the recipe is lost in the illogical logic of current time. This loss is compounded by the confusion of modern living and will require a major transformation of human thinking and subsequent changes in philosophy. Everywhere one looks they are fooled by the false promises of modern society. The basic premise is to get everybody to fall into one of two categories, the master or the servant. Of course, it is the master that determines its role and indeed the role others will play as the servant.

There is little equality in that world. The laws of that world are also designed to protect the master from those who might question this system. There is very little justice. Any sense of God that might exist is of the god of religion, the god placed before the true God, god the man, not God, The Spirit. How can there be anything spiritual in that conspiracy? It is time for the reunification of True God and humankind. It is time for equality to be re-established. It is time for the true justice of God to be re-instated. It is time for the negativity to be exposed and addressed. It is time for the change. It is time."

REUNIFICATION.

REUNIFICATION.....

1.

At this stage I was asked by my communicator to continue this series of communication under a different heading. Whereas before it was "Separation" it will continue under the heading "Reunification".

"We have shown you in our previous dissertations how negativity has and is still now constantly seeking to weaken the spiritual resolve of the human being by separating it from its strengths. Spiritual strength manifests on earth through the decisions and actions of spiritually aware people. The outcomes of these actions will be the furtherance of spiritual growth, the continuance of creation.

It must be recognised what has happened during the separation. Firstly, those people representing the element of Air were overcome by forces emanating from the point farthest from the centre of Air spirituality. *(It is my opinion that this is a reference to the Celtic invasion of Ireland, (Approx. 1500B.C.) and the subsequent history of the coming of Romanism in the form of the one known as St. Patrick, (432A.D.), Brendan).* Once conquered those who were corrupted by the negativity became the propagators of this same negativity. At the same time, these same negative forces invaded those representing the element of Water, corrupting that also. *(I take this to be the reference to the Aryan invasion of the Indus Valley.(Approx. 1500B.C), Brendan).* Next to fall to the forces of negativity were the people representing the element of the Earth. *(I take this as a reference to the "discovery" of America. (1492A.D.), Brendan),* "Finally those representing the element of Fire were subjugated to negativity and its forces. *(This being a reference to the discovery and colonisation of Australia. (1770A.D.), Brendan).*

"It will be noted that since the element of Fire was corrupted there has been an escalation in the development of a very negative aspect of humanity or should we say a rapid depletion in humanity. However, we wish to point out that part of the process of reunification will require the recognition of these events and the subsequent corruption of human thinking, human development, and human actions. It is interesting to note modern military parlance referring to "Air Power", "Ruling the Waves", "Fire Power", "Land-based troops", Air, Water, Fire, and Earth.

Fortunately, there are two elements whose people have still a strong link to their indigenous spiritual roots. These are the "People of the Earth" and the "People of Fire", the real custodians of these elements, the Native American and the Native Australian. Look to these for the means of reunification for they still have the energy of those elements held strongly.

These writings are important, especially for those who have chosen to incarnate into the land associated with the element Air. It is only Air that can again resurrect and reunify the peoples of and the powers of the other three elements. This is, therefore, the task in hand. The reason these writings need to be disseminated throughout humankind is so that each human can recognise its place in this process whether as an activist or as a supporter. Spirit needs you. God needs you.

We will give you the awareness to help you see the actions you need to take, to begin the spiritual recovery process. The only real change needed initially is a change in attitude. It is vital that each person is allowed to recognise their spiritual strength and recognise the destruction of the world they currently live in. Recognise that what has been provided for you by God through nature is being destroyed by those who have that power given to them by you entrusting your personal power to them. You are selling yourself to the "devil", becoming dependent on your "masters", to provide you at a cost, that which was freely given by God. Nature is on your side should you stand against this negativity. Remove the boundaries that separate you. Ignore the colour of the skin, the shape of the eyes or hair. See the entire human race as one and as one with all animals and at one with all nature. No one is better or lesser than another. No one is more advanced than another. All are uniquely different but equally so. No culture is better than another. No race is better than another. The love of God is in everything, in every part of God's creation. If you respect that love you will always share in that love. Reunify through and in God's Love."

Separation and Reunification of the Elements.

REUNIFICATION.....
2.

"We would remind you that the Creation of God is perfect, at least that is the hypothesis we present you with at this time. It is up to you to agree or disagree with this, to find if it is your truth or not. If God's creation is perfect then why has humankind tried to change it? What is this insane curiosity that humankind, in the form of its sciences, has for trying to create a synthetic version of what already is and at the same time decrying what already is, as being inferior to that created by a human? This is an example of the human ego in operation. Look to your forefathers for how you should live. Do not be afraid to die as part of the process. Invest your energy in living a happy life rather than in the avoidance of death. You will always die when it is the right time. Modern medicine seeks to prolong life and in order to die at the right time, it is, unfortunately, the cause of much pain and suffering to wrest the Spirit from the grasp of the ego.

119

When you encounter another human being what do you see? In most cases, you meet another's ego. When you meet what can be truly described as a spiritually aware human, in this case, you will meet their Spirit. It is unfortunate that these latter stand out as 'special' people when in fact they are normal people. The former 'ego' person is abnormal. When you meet another who is in a constant state of spiritual awareness, you will not see differences like the colour of their skin, their gender, their nationality, or their culture. You will see their Spirit. You will not see their age but will notice a clarity about them, and their true happiness. You will not hear a tale of woe and hopelessness. You will not hear a report of another's 'faults' or behaviour. You will not hear lies. You will not hear criticism. You will feel love and loved. These traits can be very difficult for the unaware human to understand and often the tendency will be for the egoist to abuse the spiritual being, for the ego to take advantage. You will have experienced the meeting of two egos and the competition that takes place. You will also have experienced meeting one who is in a state of spiritual awareness and the peace and tranquillity that can be felt, a state where trouble brings a smile rather than a grimace.

You will have met others who represent other elements than your own and who are in the awareness of who they spiritually are. You will have felt the attractiveness of their presence. This feeling is often inexplicable, more of a feeling of knowing that another had joined with you, perhaps the feeling that this other can give you some sort of support. This feeling can only occur when you are yourself aware of your own true nature and are in that consciousness when you are aware that you are in essence Spirit.

When representatives of the various elements gather together with spiritual awareness, and with a common purpose, then reunification takes place. If only two representatives get together then at least partial reunion occurs. It is important that equality is observed and that no notion of superiority or domination takes place as this will signify one or the other or both reverting to their ego and all benefit from this encounter will be nullified. It is important for all the elements to support each other and enjoy the common purpose of restoring the Spirit of Creation. Those who are busy being egoistic will feel challenged by such unification. This unification will go into every quarter of humankind. The egoism will become diluted and eventually ineffective. This will come about through the human becoming disillusioned with their religion and their society. Those that 'power' the religious and social institutions will become ineffective. Leadership will disgrace itself and a new system will be sought by the world population. It will happen that spiritual awareness will become apparent and the 'normal' reaction will not live up to the expectations of those who are in control.

Independence will become the keyword with all living within the boundaries of their own abilities. The willing recognition of the God that exists in all of creation and the respect that will be shown to that recognition will be the saving of the human race. The world of humankind is in the throes of this change at this time. Look to each other for solace. Look to the God that is in the other. See your God-likeness reflecting back upon you. Feel the Love."

Separation and Reunification of the Elements.

REUNIFICATION.....

3.

"How open are you to accepting people from other races, other cultures into your circle of friends and acquaintances? How comfortable are you sharing your life with people of different ethnicity and colour? How secure are you in sharing your opinions with others? How do you feel about the freedom for others to expressly be who they feel they are? How tolerant are you towards others? Do you see others as being difficult or challenging?

Be careful how you answer these questions. Perhaps it would be better if you didn't answer them, rather ask them of yourself without answer and see how you measure up in how you conduct yourself. This way you won't be embarrassed. Any negative reaction you express to these situations is an indication that you are not as spiritual as you thought yourself to be. It must be remembered that spirituality is about awareness, you get this awareness by observing your own reactions, and express it by your actions.

It is important that you have confidence in your association with God. It is so important to know that you have God by your side. The only way to experience God in your life is to test the hypothesis that God is indeed there. We will say that again, that God is "IN DEED" there. If you invite God into every deed you perform you will see how better it can be.

When you meet another, whoever or whatever they are, look for God in them and with them. You will often feel that the real you comes to the fore and you realise your love and compassion for the other and often also feel these qualities from them. Of course, this will require your time to be given over to this engagement, and so many people do not seem to be able to find that time. Yours is a "quick-fix" world. Humankind has lost the ability to assess and instead rushes to judge and criticise. They find any difference difficult to accept and prefer uniformity. They resist change or adventure. They suffer from boredom as a consequence and seek entertainment from unsuitable places or devices. Few realise that they are bored. The innocence of a child enables them to verbalise that feeling. It is the adult that has been conditioned not to express it. If you look at the prime entertainment of adults and see what it is doing to them, they sit in front of screens and become programmed by what they idly watch. Yes, some will watch with interest and be educated while others will watch and be entertained to relieve their boredom. Your children are being trained into the same "solution" to being bored; they are placed in front of a screen to be indoctrinated in whatever way the controllers of your world dictate. Is it any wonder then why your world is so confused? You have very little time and what time you do have for yourself you don't know what to do with it.

Your world is changing. You may think that the turmoil and segregation are negative. The world is being told to stand back and have a look at itself before it destroys itself. God will never let the world be destroyed no matter how hard humankind might try. The difficulties you face in life are those that have been created by yourselves so therefore you have the solution if only you would stand back and look and listen to your expression of your feelings, to your protestations. Having looked and listened to yourself ask yourself what are you going to do about it? You will find that your difficulty is in your inability to do much about it. This is because you have inadvertently surrendered your independence and abilities into the hands of others. You have sold your life into servitude and have no future of your own. You are only part of the future of another. When they retire many people age rapidly and die of boredom.

See life as the adventure it is. It is a spiritual adventure, each new day presenting a fresh set of challenges and excitements for you. This can be as simple as disrupting your plans but in doing so giving you a fresh set of opportunities. You can only really rise to these occasions when you have spiritual awareness, where you can see what God's law has in store for you. We will remind you of the Law and how everything is as a consequence of what went before it? The wisdom that can be gained from this law is the wisdom for the future. What appears to be a negative outcome, when it is made positive becomes this wisdom. When this negativity is not transmuted it remains the ignorance of the present. This is why we suggest that life can be challenging and exciting.

You will probably find this strange but those in this world relish the opportunity and challenge of incarnating into your world and willingly volunteer to take on the role that is required of them in order to implement a future for the continued growth of Spirit and the expansion of creation. We in Spirit are observing you at all times and guiding you to where you need to be. We can only do this when you are in harmony with our consciousness, spiritual consciousness, and free of the distractions that negative or ego consciousness places in your way. Go now in God's Love."

REUNIFICATION.....

4.

"We can see the world of humankind is well on the way to its reunification. Firstly, humankind needs to reunify itself. Next, it needs to reunite with its nature and then reunite with nature itself. Humankind has separated from each other, even to its genders separating.

Gender difference is what makes unification possible; the natural attraction one gender has for the other. We see the gender issues in your world raising complex scenarios that really have no basis when one can accept another for who they truly are. There is too much confusion being created through the misunderstanding of the nature of gender and sex, just as there is confusion between love and sex. There is a tendency to assume the attraction one human feels for another is sexual. Similarly, when one feels the love from another the tendency is to assume that there is sex somewhere involved. Of course, this is not only confined to male-female encounters but it does suggest that the human doesn't understand its own feelings.

This insensitivity to what one's feelings are telling them is a major cause of alienation amongst humans. When one cannot trust their own feelings how then can they trust another? Automatically your feelings will present themselves in every situation you encounter. They are always there. The human has become so adept at ignoring them and so unaccustomed at utilising them, that negativity can completely control your actions and responses. This negativity works through your ego. When you find yourself reacting to any situation then you will see what we are referring to.

Without knowledge of your feelings, how else would you know the difference between loving attraction and sexual attraction? How can you know the difference between your attractions to the opposite or similar gender? This feeling could be also described as an appetite seeking to be satisfied. Think of how you feel around food. You feel the hunger and the need to eat. Even in this, you might have a longing for particular foods to satisfy that particular appetite. Now think of the hunger that one might have for love. Here too there can be a need for particular ingredients. In this case, we will use the term relationship. What type of relationship are you seeking? What are you interpreting your feelings to be telling you? One needs to be aware of what their feelings are telling them. One of the most powerful driving forces in the human being is its ego. As you will know from previous writings when spiritual awareness is not nourished ego manifests. Love is a Divine attribute and love attraction is a spiritual experience. It is the Spirit of one recognising the Spirit of another. This recognition is irrespective of gender, race, or creed.

It can even be irrespective of species. This is unification in its truest sense.

Animals of other species recognise it, so why not the human animal? Within nature, there are certain protocols to be observed, so too with human nature. These rules are very simple and obvious to the thinking mind of humankind. The unfortunate thing is that the human mind seldom thinks, especially before it sends out the order to act. With many aboriginal peoples thinking before action is commonplace. It is in Western Society that reaction comes first. This is so common that the chaos that ensues drives people apart. Differences become an obstacle for unity instead of being an attraction. The world would not exist if this were a common feature of all species. This is why humankind is killing its world.

These days people are being driven into an encounter with each other. This is the positive side of the negative activities of the dominant society. It is the destruction of humankind that will be its saving. This might sound strange, but let me explain. As has been said before, "things only get as bad as they need to get, before they improve". When situations get really bad the human turns to its creator. The child turns to its parent, and the parent turns to God. When that happens, the correct change can take place. There is a proviso, however, and that is the ability or sensitivity of the human being able to correctly read its feelings and acting accordingly.

We started these writings by illustrating how poorly equipped modern human is to understand their own feelings. How then are we to communicate with you so you will become better tuned to God's assistance? Firstly, you need to call on God for that help. Don't direct your call to anyone else, neither to me, your own guide, or an angel. You, by realising your failings and calling directly to God will invoke an immediate response. That response will always be appropriate but you need to clear the way to let is manifest. This is where your guides come into action. Spirit guides firstly have to take on a soul mantle so they are more familiar to your inexperienced mind. This is why we are doing these writings so that your mind can be opened by them and returned into spiritual awareness. In this guise, they will adopt an acceptable form to assist you. You might find that they will impress upon your friends or acquaintances and use them as an intermediary. In your darkest hour, your 'knight in shining armour' will appear with God's help.

In order for this to be of positive benefit, the correct mindset has to be adopted. If the situation has gotten so bad that Divine intervention is required then some clearing needs to be done. By this, we mean that your mind must be clear of negative thought and that you have resigned yourself to understanding your place in that world. Your place is a Spirit with a body that is in distress seeking God's help. You need to surrender yourself to this assistance and be prepared to act upon it when it arrives. Always remember, "Miracles only occur in miraculous places". A miraculous place is one devoid of negativity. Your surrender to God's assistance clears all negativity.

If you are experiencing hardship and seek to change your circumstances, heed these words and test their veracity and give God a call."

# *REUNIFICATION.....*

5.

"All that is beneficial to spiritual development, where the journey that Spirit will take through the earthly or material realms is concerned, has already been put in place through the foresight of the Creator. If one is to look at all other species and observe the interdependency one has upon the other, it will be noted that there is perfect harmony. Each element knows its place and how to function as the being it is. It is a perfect system.

The world of peace and harmony radically changed with the advent of humankind. Where all that existed before this event worked in harmony and interdependency it did not have free will. All was based on an instinctive cycle. It was not influenced by any negativity as no negativity existed. God cannot create any negativity; God can only create goodness.

Again, we refer to the Book of Genesis and the myth of Adam and Eve. If we are to look at what this myth portrays, it tells the story of the giving of form, of life, and of free will to a new species now known as humankind. We have discussed in earlier communications how the first humans sought power in the form of knowledge, even though they had been told that knowledge was not for them. It tells of the consequence of power seeking. One might think that this is merely a story; however, it is a story but a story that contains a very strong lesson, a story that must not be dismissed.

You might think that as this was so very long ago that it no longer has any value. Do you not realise that this quest for power is still going on within all human societies in one form or another, but particularly in western society? It is a quest for power for powers sake only, and not for the general good of humankind, or the good of any other species on the planet earth. It is this quest for power that is the greatest cause of separation.

In these times it is increasingly obvious that those in power are mere puppets to the created negativity of humankind. The free will conferred on the human form has been usurped by the egotistical few who have wrested power from the meek and humble. These few have taken God's creation and corralled it for their own use. They trade it for the power of the meek. Ask yourself who owns the land? Who owns the oceans and rivers? Who owns the sky and the air? Who owns the sun, moon and the stars? Surely these are all the property of the One who created it? Surely all belongs to God, including you? This is how negative your society has become. This is how negative your fundamental thinking has been trained into performing, performing for these corrupt and spiritually illegal systems that have been put in place to control human behaviour. Is it any wonder why there is so much sickness in your world? All illness is a gift from God to provide the necessary guidance back to the right path. Your society seeks to develop treatments that will help you ignore the message the illness carries and enables you to keep on the wrong path and in subservience to the few. Nothing can improve until these facts are realised and acted upon.

Reunification cannot begin until the boundaries are recognised and removed. Many of these boundaries are almost indiscernible because of the preoccupation with the hunger for power that is instilled in every human by the society it is born into. People are encouraged to look to the apparent success of others and to compare themselves to it, to see how they 'shape up'.

Everybody has their own power. This power is the power they need to travel the journey of development for their Spirit and consequently of The Spirit. God created you and the world that way. Should you gain in power it is only at the loss of power of another. Yes, you can grow more powerful but only spiritually so, and never through the loss of another. Spiritual power is awareness; more spiritual power is the increase in awareness.

We have raised questions for you to ask yourself, such as who owns the land. If you want to continue to live, who do you have to buy your living from? Why do you have to buy it? By what means do you pay for it? Now ask yourself if you can see another way, another way without selling your soul."

Separation and Reunification of the Elements.

REUNIFICATION.....

6.

"Corruption is all about power. Social power is measured by financial wealth. Financial power is in the power to earn and the power to buy and sell. We ended our last dissertation mentioning selling your soul, and yet your Spirit can never be sold. Your Spirit is coupled to your physical being for the duration of its life on earth. Many humans fail to realise that the soul can outlive the physical body if it chooses or if it is in a state of unawareness. It is often found that those who sold their body into bondage also inadvertently sold their soul. This contract they entered into can continue after physical death.

If one were to be reared within a traditional indigenous system, they would learn all the skills necessary to survive without the need for money. They would learn independent living. Of course, these times there would be the problem of buying a place to live and finding a place where one could freely forage. If one were to live naturally, society would make them outcasts, social misfits. In other words people who are socially unfit. That is the inhumanity of modern human society. Indigenous people do not have the currency to purchase freedom from the limitations so-called western society imposes upon them. The modern social system sets the boundaries, and gives instructions to its citizens. These citizens are those who have entered into a contract with the governing body of the state they are born into. The unfortunate new-born becomes a registered member of a state, and of a religion, before they are reason-abled. They are not allowed choice even though it is their own Divine right. The system then streamlines them into servitude and hopelessness. They become hopeless of ever being free again and in order to survive acquiesce to the dictates of those who have usurped their power. Many feel the only way they can escape this confinement is to take back their power. They mistakenly tear up the contract by taking their life back and terminating it. This is an act of despair, an act of hopelessness, an act of defiance, and most of all a quest for freedom. The irony is that they see the only way to live freely is to die.

Of course, taking one's own life is never the answer spiritually. In spiritual terms it is not a sin. Mind you when they find themselves in this world the unawareness is lifted and they are again exposed to their awareness, and then they realise they had only advanced a short distance along their path. With this realisation they will seek a return to earth at the earliest opportunity. This opportunity generally only presents itself when those on earth, who would hope they would meet them on their own physical demise, manage to do so. As there is no time in Spirit, they will find this time passes quickly, and they will be able to reincarnate and resume their earthly journey.

It is hoped that through these writings, and all the others that are being transmitted into your world, will make a profound change, so that when these Spirits reincarnate the world will be a different and better place. At this time spiritual development has all but stalled and is in need of a restart. You will notice how we in Spirit are doing all we can to show you the folly of your ways. We are also inspiring solutions. One of the foremost points we seek to make is that the reunification of humankind is of paramount importance. The gulf between the "haves" and the "have-nots" is ever increasing. In a world where all are meant to be equal, this is very disturbing. The gulf between humankind and nature is also increasing alarmingly. These gulfs can be bridged only if you can afford it financially.

It would appear that those in power would hope there is no God. The only God those in power know is a God of wrath, a God to be feared. They build edifices to this God in the hope of atonement. But this is the false God and it can never stand up to the Law of Cause and Effect. The sacrifice they make to this God is the annihilation of humankind, not realising they too are part of humanity, and equally at risk. Humankind can live on the provisions God has created for them, as God created for all life. If humankind can find the way to live with God and reject the system those currently in power seek to impose upon them, then there is a future.

God's plan was a paradise; humankind turned it into a hell. Revert now to God's plan and be happy and fulfilled. Life then is a blessing from God for those who choose to live it, free and happy."

Separation and Reunification of the Elements.

REUNIFICATION.....

7.

"These writings appear to some as being anti-political and anti-religion, this is not our intention. It is difficult to identify the difference, as both religion and politics are designed to wrest the power from the individual and more importantly from God. These elements, over the millennia, have created such a screen between God and humankind that in order to talk to you about spirituality it is necessary to penetrate this screen and therefore to discuss how this screen exists and to give you an awareness of it.

The Spirit existed before humankind, indeed before everything that it has subsequently created. You might ask who created the Spirit? The answer to that question doesn't exist. However, if you were to ask how Spirit was created, you might get an answer. There is a difficulty here too. No human has encountered or languaged the composition of any Spirit, never mind the Master Creator. At this time Spirit remains incomprehensible to the human mind. Suffice to say, the only way to understand God is to be God-like. In this way, you can experience what it is. If you like, being God-like is being spiritually aware, and has nothing to do with thinking you are God. Yes, you are part of the composition and must find your place. As you develop your spiritual awareness you will automatically find that place where you belong. This might sound as if we are trying to avoid the question; however, if you fail to understand what we are saying it is obvious to us you are not yet capable of receiving the answer.

The evidence of God is all around you. You are more than likely to have even experienced your God-likeness today. Have you felt grateful for life today? Have you appreciated how you have been facilitated in surviving another day? Are you looking forward to tomorrow? Have you realised how this day has given you a fresh opportunity of there being a future for you? If you cannot answer yes to all of these questions then you can accept you are not open to spiritual awareness. If you find an excuse for avoiding how wonderful life and living is, if you fail to take responsibility for every choice you make, then you are not living through your Divine Being. You are living, like so many do in a state of ego consciousness. You are not being God-like. You might think we are judging you, whereas we are only giving you the tools to judge yourself.

Why then are you finding it difficult to be in a state of spiritual awareness? This is where politics and religion come into our discussion. The answer to this particular question is simple, you have been trained, conditioned, programmed, call it what you will, to be engrossed in your physicality and your spiritual awareness has been replaced by religious awareness. Even this latter is better than nothing, and the way society is currently going is further into nothingness.

Change is certainly coming to your world, like it or not. There are strong movements in the thinking of humankind. The false Gods that have been the effigies that humankind has subscribed to are falling. The apparent stability that these Gods afforded to human life has now turned out to be a quagmire. This quagmire was hidden by the thin crust of materialism. Nothing can prevent the instability that is in your world today except God consciousness, spiritual awareness. Through the use of spiritual awareness, stability can be restored to your life. Spiritual awareness is easy to achieve. You shouldn't need these writings, but apparently, you must do.

Remember we are here by invitation. We are aware of the insecurity humankind is experiencing due to the transition that is taking place. It is said, "Old habits die hard". Your habits go back many generations, and that makes it harder still. Many are the prayers seeking an intervention in the trials and tribulations that humankind is confronted by.

We are here to help you in any way we can. We are here in the name of God, and we also pray. We pray for the strength in our own minds to help transmute the negativity in the human mind into positive growth and understanding. All we ask in return is that you listen to our words, listen with an open mind. In the awareness this can give you, you will be able then to make up your own mind. God blesses you."

Separation and Reunification of the Elements.

REUNIFICATION.....

8.

"Just because you do not realise the wonderful world God has created for you, you have no right to disregard and destroy it. Within nature there is a remedy for every illness, but not for those illnesses created by humankind. We have spoken before as to humankind being the source for all evil, or as we would prefer to call it negative ignorance. Positivity can also have ignorance; we call that unawareness. There is no excuse for not wanting to know, for not wanting awareness. How often we hear the human utter that they don't want to know, or that they didn't ask for this or that. Spirit is always willing to help you advance your awareness, but you have to be prepared to surrender your ignorance. Somehow humankind appears to have difficulty with doing that.

It is said, "Ignorance is bliss" and, "It's a folly to be wise". It is interesting, for if these quotations are accurate and used it can become a mantra for those who continue to resist our subtle lessons in becoming more aware, and we have to resort to more and less subtle notifications drawing your attention to that which you lack. Of course, our motivation it totally at the behest of the Supreme, at the behest of, and under the instruction of God, and solely for your benefit. The basic human needs are simple, food in your stomach, clothes on your back, a roof over your head, and of course the means to serve these needs. God in Creation has provided for these needs. If God hadn't then humankind would have ceased to exist long ago. Isn't this a profound revelation? You can read about so many cases of survival, where the survivor survived shipwreck on a life raft in the middle of the ocean, on a deserted island, in the arid desert, in the frozen wastes. In each case, they had to rely on instinct and nature. Unfortunately, credit for their survival is often attributed to the great efforts of the rescuers and not to the God-given instincts and the useable nature that was Divinely provided.

There is another trait of the human, the role of the "rescuer". When the 'power game' is examined, it will be found that the average human of these times is totally unaware of this 'games' existence. In other communications, we have discussed this topic from time to time. Being 'rescued' in many situations unconsciously undermines one's confidence in one's self. This undermining is in fact due to depowerment, especially when one doesn't ask to be rescued. If one is to ask for assistance, it becomes empowerment. Note we carefully use the word 'rescue' in parenthesis and assistance without them. The difference is the loss of power or the gaining of power. It is an indication of your power when you realise the need for assistance and a further indication of your power when you overcome your ego and request it. Spirit will never undermine your confidence by taking away your difficulty. Spirit will assist you by encouraging you to make the necessary decisions and to inspire you to have the strength to implement the plan that will resolve the issue. Spirit will let you experience and use the power you were born with and will help you regain any power you may have given to others or given to bothersome situations.

Everybody in every species has the right to its life, the right to sustain its life, and the right to end its life. In the last situation, should the body have spiritual awareness the end of life will be calm and natural, and not before its time. In the world of these times, there is a general lack of spiritual awareness and consequently, the end of life is not seen as a pleasant prospect. This human preoccupation with sustaining life draws suffering and often drastic methods being employed to wrest the soul and Spirit from the grasp of the ego. In the cut and thrust of the 'power game,' the suppression of spiritual awareness is achieved by the depowerment of the ego. The ego is educated into a dependency upon the system it is to live within. The ego sees its only hope of survival is to live by the rules that the state dictates, even when it is called a democracy. The only hope it sees for its spiritual survival is its reliance on the religion it is born into, or chooses to convert to. When the Spirit incarnates into a human form it is dependent on its human parents for its physical survival. This dependency required this incarnation to surrender its power to its parents. This power is only entrusted to the parent(s) until such time as the child becomes self-sufficient. At this stage, the youth should have its power returned to it, and then continue to grow and develop increasingly, under its own power. If its power has been returned its prospects for fulfilment will be perfect. However, if this power is retained by the parent(s) there is no such surety as to its future. This underpowered individual would next be exposed to the ruthlessness of society. Their life is now subjective. Any apparent self-confidence is but a veneer and any assertive acts are simply egotistical bravado. Yes, they can survive but only through the care of the system. The next loss of power they experience is when they find they need to further subjugate themselves to the available educational and financial services, and of course to those who would give them employment. This will be dealt with in more detail later.

All are born into this world of yours fully spiritually aware. All are born fully powered. All are born equal. All are born into the world of humankind. All are born perfectly equipped for the life that is ahead of them. It is this need to surrender your early lives to your parent(s) and their unawareness to hand it back that presents all future difficulties you will encounter. This situation you find yourself in has been predetermined by you prior to your incarnating. It is nobody's fault there is no one to blame. There is a situation to be resolved and resolved by you and nobody else. Ultimately only you have that power. Re-find that power and truly live, it is there waiting for you to take back. You are not alone in your quest; we are always with you. There is no difficulty so great, as long as it's your difficulty, that you lack the power to overcome. Of course, there is always the exception. In this situation, should you have given your power to another you will need to turn to them for them to use the power that is really yours to solve your difficulty. If and when the difficulty is resolved it is they who will get the praise and the benefit that is rightly rewarding your power. You will be left feeling unhappy and unfulfilled, even though you will be relieved that the problem has gone away. You will also give thanks to this other, further empowering them with more of what is yours.

You might ask us now how this anomaly can be resolved? Our answer as always is simple, by becoming aware, trusting that we are there helping you, accepting that all is within your control, and then setting about correcting the situation. The solution is the correct action. The correct action is within your knowing. Your knowing is accessed through awareness. This is the awareness that we offer you in these writings. God blesses you."

Separation and Reunification of the Elements.

REUNIFICATION.....

9.

"All are children of the one God, you and we. We too are of God, as is every living thing. You might think this strange to think, though inanimate doesn't mean un-living. Once created everything is of its creator. The human is created by its parents but it is God that gives it life. The pot is created by the potter; it is the potters Spirit that gives the pot that different feeling when you use it. Machines also make pots but machine-made pots feel different to the user than potter made pots. Everything created is imbued with the Spirit of its creator, and that Spirit gives it life. Back to the potter made pot; have you noticed how when you break it you feel the loss? You are feeling that its life has gone; its Spirit is there no longer.

Humans brand everybody that is not of the human world an alien. Yes, you call us Spirits, or souls, or ghosts depending on your awareness. In reality, we are often considered to be aliens and should we manifest in your world the 'rational' human mind seeks to give us form and applies some description that satisfies the mind, hence the various titles that are applied. When you do this application, you create an image that is familiar to you but alien to us. When you visit our world in your meditation, we see your soul form. Were it not for our awareness we would label you alien. When the human has awareness, sufficient spiritual awareness to not need to impose a form upon us, we can appear as Spirit. Therefore, what separates us is lack of awareness. Lack of awareness can be called ignorance, so we are separated only by ignorance.

Many still insist on calling the Spirit, soul, and the soul, Spirit. These people are unaware. Many confuse psychic mediumship with spiritual mediumship. The difference is only a matter of consciousness, and the psychic has merely not awakened to Spirit yet. This is not to say that the psychic is not working correctly and doing their job. The role of a psychic medium is similar to being an apprentice, when the apprenticeship is completed, they may become a spiritual medium. This was the role originally imagined by Spirit, unfortunately, egos get in the way at the first glimpse of communication with worlds other than the Earth; communication with beings other than human beings. In the development of this medium, we had to start somewhere, so we started with the tangible personality of the being who had been incarnate and was called Webb. The Spirit that had incarnated in Webb and gave that body life, is now back in human form. That Spirit is now this medium......."*(I must say I'm shocked by this revelation; I had never thought of that one. B.)*

REUNIFICATION.....

10.

(As I sit to write this, I feel it different from before. I would normally sit and allow my communicator to take over and do all the writing for me. Now, however, I can feel the presence of the communicator and at the same time, I have a sense of a different relationship with them. I feel more a part of the team. It's as if I'm more involved in these writings. I still haven't fully adjusted to the revelation in Reunification 9. B)

"Reunification requires action on the part of those who wish to reunify. We have seen how this medium has reunified their being; their body mind and Spirit are now one again. In previous communications, we have described how the separation begins at birth and continues until it becomes a natural behaviour for the separated to be all about ego, the body and the mind, and very little, if any, about the Spirit. Most religions relegate pseudo-religious practices to a weekend day and other odd days throughout the year. Many of these 'odd days', such as Christmas day, have been chosen by religion so as to mask the true nature of these special times in the lives of humankind.

An important part of the reunification process is to reinstate within your mind, an understanding of the elements and an understanding of these special days in the natural calendar. Humankind is an intrinsic part of nature and cannot hope to survive without reassuming its place within creation. Every aspect of creation has its purpose in order for the Earth, and the world that lives on it, to continue. At this time the balance between a future for your world or the destruction of your world is favouring further destruction. The air is polluted, the water is polluted, and the earth is dying. Only fire remains with any strength, and that is the final frontier. We have told you before that God would never allow humankind to destroy the earth. Humankind has now reached the point where Spirit will have to step in and protect its creation, even at the cost of humankind. No other species in your world has the destructive nature of the human. The human thinks it is the superior species, but it is not. Where humankind is concerned, it is the only species that can and will rebel against God. What do you think this last statement means? It suggests that humankind has to work harder to maintain a relationship with God and be, like other species, closer to God in thought word and deed. Humankind needs to reunite with its spiritual nature, resume its spiritual journey and shun the negativity that operates through the human ego.

Learn how to use and work with the elements. Learn to live through the understanding that other species exercise. Learn to observe your actions, and more importantly your reactions. Realise your spirituality and how comfortably it fits into this wonderful world of yours when correctly understood. Go now to ponder these words. Be open to receiving God's blessings."

REUNIFICATION.....

11.

"At this time, the human is in all cases a fractured being, except for the minority of indigenous societies that have maintained the knowledge of self-sufficiency and the ability to sustain them in a Godly manner. This means they have not sold their lives to others; they have maintained their independence. They are not slaves to the "system" or the religion of others.

The key here is not only self-sufficiency but also self-sustainability. While this can be achieved independently it is better to be interdependent, to be a community where those that 'can' help those that 'can't'. Those who can't will always have something they can contribute to others, even if it is only their innocence, or their wisdom, or their memory, or their love and support to those that can.

Everybody has some feature, some unique skill to contribute to their community. As humanity is a part of the creation plan it needs to take its place by integrating with all other aspects of their God purpose, to be God-like. Some try to be God! It is your duty to you yourself to realise what your purpose is and to seek to achieve that purpose and to be fulfilled.

There are many inventions created by inspired humans that are designed to assist you in life. Someone invented fire for example, and others invented quicker ways of lighting those fires. Someone invented the wheel, and others invented ways of making it turn. Both of these examples required inspiration. The initial inspiration would have been there to help humankind; the secondary inventions would have been to speed up the potential productivity of the primary inventions. The need to speed up the process is so that time can be gained. Time is a fixed measurement and cannot be wasted nor gained. It merely passes. By shortening any process is essentially removing it from a natural application of time, God time, and into a controlled time of humankind. Human time in societal terms has a monetary value and is, therefore, a commodity. To save human time is to increase the productive time. In the modern social structure, this saved time is then allocated to the goal of making more money, perhaps even by the labouring class having more time to give to the manufacture of more time saving devices, so more people will have the time to design more devices for them to produce, to save more time?

Doesn't this sound strange? People these times, do not even have the time to rear their own offspring. Those who have the time see fit to employ others to look after their children, so they can pursue the unnatural life of earning money and yet more money just so they can enjoy the time-saving devices. We see this as being the great folly in human thinking. What do you see it as? If you understand what we are illustrating by these words, you will have no answer to this question. If you have an answer, then it is but an excuse and you are one of the deluded.

This is the dilemma that is facing humankind and is both a spiritual and physical conundrum. It is this difficulty that is leading to the extinction of not only human life but possibly to all life on that planet. Only one species stands any chance of survival and that is the plant kingdom. Plants can regenerate on the corpse of any body, and those plants have a Divine quotient, a Spirit. This Spirit is in the physical world of the Earth with a purpose and will give unquestionable devotion to its creator, to God, and respect to all other living aspects of that creation. Why is it that the other equally important part of creation cannot be like this? Why cannot humankind reunify their own being, Spirit, body and mind, offering the same unquestioning devotion to The Creator, to God, and respect all other aspects of that Creation? In doing this they will be self-sufficient and self-sustainable. There is also the bonus of being happy and fulfilled and worry-less."

Separation and Reunification of the Elements.

REUNIFICATION.....

12.

"It is important in the process of reunification that the normal behaviour of the human is in accordance with its form as it was first created. As with every element of creation it was carefully designed for a certain purpose. This awareness of purpose has been lost, especially in the last millennia. There have been many reinventions of the human form, each designed to suit the next phase of its existence. No creation has ever failed, and having achieved its goal went through the process of extinction and reinvention. This current human form has a long road ahead of it yet before it reaches its conclusion. Be assured God will see to that.

Every Spirit that is currently incarnate has been through several of those previous humanoid forms even though they have no memory of such. The world is so different that to have memory of those times would be detrimental rather than advantageous. Such is the difference between the then and now that there would be little relevance in this knowing. If you are to look at how the current generations of humankind fails to appreciate the wisdom of its elders, never mind the lessons of the past of this current human form, you can therefore understand how lacking in any benefit would be the memory and wisdom to be gleaned from times past.

We would stress that the understanding of the 'why' of creation is important. As in every case Spirit suggests that humanity needs to question and there is always the human who seeks to supply the answer. Why can you not be content to leave the energy of the question and await the energy of the answer to evolve? If the answer were already known then there would be no need for the question. If you like every question is but a key to the door of evolving creation. It is in the seeking of the answer that life has a purpose, a purpose that will eventually lead to further questions and a future reason for humankind to continue its existence.

These times in your world there is constant conflict. One might ask why this is? We see this as the collective negativity of the human ego resisting the inevitable realisation that life has little to do with the human temporary physical form and solely to do with the incumbent Spirit. These conflicts achieve nothing other than to delay the process, which of course serves negativity. In Spirit there is no measurement of time and delay does not affect the Spirit in any way. Who knows how many steps the Spirit has chosen to take in its incarnation? In fact, it is not the number of steps its body takes but the achievement of its purpose for that lifetime that counts. Can we say, no Spirit withdraws from the body until that purpose has been achieved? Every event in that life has been a means towards the successful conclusion of life. Death is merely the means of shedding the physical body and releasing the Spirit contained safely within its protective soul body. Though released from its physical restraints does not mean the conflict ends. As the soul body is the etheric physical body double it comprises the remains of the ego. Should the human being have died while engrossed in its ego side of life and not have the spiritual awareness to help it understand its new existence, it will create a life similar to the one it has just left. Of course, it will have the ability to connect to those whom it loved whilst incarnate but it will be a very disconnected relationship. Should those loved ones also lack spiritual awareness it will be very difficult for the recently departed to gain any solace from these encounters. In their life they had led a life where their ego side was separated from their Spiritual side. This separation was 'artificially' induced, often through the dependencies that were developed through a deluded and misinformed upbringing, in other words a false reality. Death separates the ego from the false premise that human society offers and leaves it unsupported. On dying separation from reality becomes real.

The first step in reunification therefore, is the reunification of the body and the Spirit, preferably while still in the physical world. If this doesn't happen it is not then the "end of the world". (How many of these ancient sayings are very wise and spiritually appropriate). This saying tells us that though we might be dead and unfulfilled it is not the end of the world for the ego and that it still has time for the reconciliation with its Spirit to occur. Once this happens the ego will cease to exist, except in the minds and thoughts of those it knew and that are still incarnate. This is why if you have a relative or friend pass away it is important you think kindly of them and especially remember their unique and special attributes. This will greatly assist the ego in surrendering to its positivity and surrendering to its spiritual nature, the reunification of body and Spirit. Naturally this should be an easier process when one is still in the physical world. It should be, but then why isn't it? The answer is simply that the world of the human no longer places the necessary respect and time into realising its spiritual side. The human is educated to ignore their spiritual function and therefore does not nurture it adequately. It is important to respect the body from a spiritual perspective and to educate the human ego to respect its Spirit and to ensure there is no conflict."

REUNIFICATION.....

13.

"Having first reunified one's self, the next stage of reunification is the mind, body and Spirit of the family. The family unit has been formed through the process of Divine Creation. Though one might think that God had very little to do with it, the family, like the individual, has been an inspired formation. Each individual Spirit has used its free will to participate in this union and no matter which role they play, it has always been in accordance with the Divine Will.

The roles chosen are very important for the individual to recognise as this will enable them to understand their duty. In these times there is very little understanding in the area of human intercourse, especially so when it comes to human sexual intercourse. In other dissertations we have spoken about love. We have explained how true love is not linked to sex. Sex has a purpose but does not deserve to status that modern humanity places upon it. By elevating sex to such an important role in human intercourse has attracted the attention of the negative aspects of the ego and delegated this act into the armoury of tools used by negativity to divide the natural powers of the human. This has introduced an ignorance of the individual roles of the human and based the human functionality on gender roles rather than the many other aspects of an individual human. The sexes become redefined and their roles in modern society misunderstood. Their individual ability becomes limited and very restricted. In these days, however, humanity has moved past that phase, though having passed it, does not have the understating to fill the void that has been developed as a consequence. The female becomes more masculine and the male becomes more feminine. The process of forming a family relationship under this ignorance is doomed to disappointment.

When the awareness of there being a gender difference occurs in the developing child it is important that the parents carefully nurture this awareness. Too often the adults are to busy in their own confusion to offer any guidance to the child, and would sooner leave that to others to nurture and guide them. This never works. If it doesn't happen in the home it will never healthily happen outside the home. There will be a perpetual cycle of unnatural development leading to dysfunctional misbehaviour. Unfortunately, this dysfunctionality has become the norm for Western society and the negativity that is countering positivity has been allowed to triumph. It has succeeded in division amongst the building blocks of human behaviour. This has created the insensitive, compassion lacking, selfish, individual prepared to remain in its ignorance rather than accept the challenges of life that will give it the opportunity of discovering who they truly are, and their purpose for being in human life. They lose the ability to recognise the perfect choices they made prior to becoming incarnate, to become the human individual they are and to use the positivity of these choices to fulfil the role they came to manifest and experience.

One might well ask, and it is hoped they will, what is it all about? The only answer is to live your life and see. You will only see the enlightenment that human life can provide through the understanding of the experiences you have caused to occur in your life through your choices. If you have chosen through your ignorance the outcome will be unsavoury. If you choose through your awareness the outcome will be truly enjoyable. You will remember the basic rule, "If it makes you happy, do it. If it makes you unhappy, don't do it." If you feel a situation is unkind to you, it is important to realise that no matter what might appear to be contributing factors, it has still been as a consequence of a choice you made sometime previously, maybe even before your current incarnation. You chose to be born into the world of matter. You chose the best route for accessing what you needed in that world. It can then be seen that not only did you choose those who would provide you with the physical body but you also chose who you would like to share life with. You chose your family. They in their individuality chose you also.

The family unit therefore is the consequences of the spiritual choices of perfect individuals. Any dysfunction with the family is a reflection of the subtle interference of negativity, often manifested through the ego of the individuals comprising that family being in conflict, commonly referred to as sibling rivalry. This rivalry is often unconsciously created through the unaware actions and responses of the parents. The parents in their turn have been conditioned by their parents and influenced by their upbringing. There is no blame to be apportioned to any parent as each are chosen for the quality of life they bring into the life of their child, no matter how negative that might appear. You have chosen to be in the family to share in the chosen experiences of others and to gain the awareness this can afford you. You will only get the positive benefit of these experiences should you take this responsibility onto yourself. The contribution that each member of a family makes into the spiritual development of each other can only be seen after the event and never seen during the dynamics of the process. This also applies to life; it is only at the end of it that one can appreciate all that has happened to them and the appropriateness of it all.

Your family, whether it includes siblings or not, is an important unit. If it remains intact or separates it is how it is meant to be. The bond that is there is a bond of love. If there is separation there is no loss once true love exists, not even the loss of life. In death the human grieves the loss of the life, but the Spirit always enjoys the bond of love.

Then there is the greater extended family, the uncles, the aunts, the cousins no matter how many times removed are all a part of this amazing unit in the human world. If just one individual in that unit can maintain spiritual awareness then there is hope that their influence can heal all the ignorance that might prevail in their generation. Everybody, consciously or unconsciously, hungers for spiritual food, hungers to have God in their lives. The family unit is sacred and therefore so often the target for negativity to create disharmony amongst the members, the human element, the ego and its ignorance, will be part of this negative play. The reunified individual within this family will provide the catalyst for God to direct the light of awareness into the midst. It is hoped that the awareness of that one individual will heal any rifts that exist amongst the other members and peace love and harmony can coexist within this precious unit. The family is then unified."

REUNIFICATION.....

14.

"The task of reunification gets more difficult the wider the scope of that which needs to be reunified is recognised. It will be remembered that when this compilation of writings began, we spoke of the separation of the fundamental elements of your world. According to one of the myths of creation as told in The Book of Genesis, it began with the human quest for ultimate power, the fruit from the tree of knowledge, and later in the biblical stories of the children of Adam and Eve, Cain and Able, separating because of their sibling rivalry with Cain eventually murdering Able. It could be said that this is the first record of murder. It also illustrates denial and lies being used to avoid responsibility and punishment. However, this is a myth, but then all myths carry a moral and this moral is to be aware of lusting for power in any form.

It can be seen that whatever the origin of this myth it is ancient wisdom. It is illustrating a situation that to this day has not been heeded nor resolved. These divisions created by the need for the supremacy of the individual are still very much alive within all areas of society and are growing daily.

If one is but to look at one's self and to see how we are behaving towards our fellows, if we are honest, we will see that we have serious shortcomings. There is so much concern regarding titles, Mr., Ms., Sir, Madam, Dr., etc, and these just before your name, and then there are the letters one seeks to add behind their name, PhD., etc. Where then is there the acceptance of the simple Tom, Dick, or Harriet? Where then is there the opportunity of meeting the uniqueness of the individual? The individual has been pre-assessed by their title and given a degree of respect that they might not deserve. If one is to learn not to be impressed by title then they will not give away power to it. In modern society the abuse of this power so generously given to those with title is prevalent. Look at the trust that is given to various authorities and how many of those so entrusted abuse their position for personal gain and often at a cost to those who empowered them. This could be called blind faith, or even a faith held by those who have been blinded or fooled by the lies and deceit emanating from the mouths of those who hide behind the guise of title.

If one is to evaluate the individual by their actions then one will be less likely to be fooled. Look to the actions of those who you allow to have power over you and see are they worthy of the position you hold them in. Look for the God aspect within every human being and see how deep within them do you have to look. If it isn't immediately visible then reserve your power and do not part with any of it before you have a clear sight of how it will be used. Democracy has everyone fooled into parting with their personal power. Humankind has surrendered itself into a dictatorship through it dependency of those it has no control over. The greed, and power quest of many individuals has brought in an authority in most parts of your world that is inherently corrupt, and acting in its own interests, without fear of retribution from those who have conferred their power upon them. This is causing separation within families and indeed within communities. We have spoken about the reunification of the individual and the self-empowerment that is natural within everybody. We have spoken regarding how that power is lost. We have spoken of the reunification of the individual with their family and indeed the reunification of the family unit, and how powerful that unit is. Now let us talk about the reunification of the community. A community is a conglomeration of families. A community is composed of all the ingredients to be potentially self-sufficient. It is a unit that has existed since the advent of humankind, and is designed by God. In some societies these conglomerates may be called tribes. Every skill necessary for the continued existence of humankind, within the framework of Creation exists within the community. The difficulties arise when the members of the community stop freely sharing their individual skills. Humankind has developed many devices to take the labour out of living but has also developed a whole new supply chain. They have developed a different form of labour, that which produces labour saving devices. Free time has become so precious and scarce that more devices are required to make more time available, more time to make more devices, and on it goes. If one were to step back and to observe how much time is wasted in saving more time to waste, one would see the silly anomaly that exists. It is said, "The only pressure is time". Time as measured in hours and minutes is an invention of humankind. In ancient times it was measured by "when is the right time", if you like true God time. Spiritually time is a sequence of events, one event leading to another subsequent event. If you like the Law of Cause and Effect, Karma, Continuous

Creation, or whatever you wish to call it is God time. To use God time correctly it is first necessary to understand one's individual needs and service those need. Secondly one needs to observe one's unique position within its family and how it can best responsibly serve that position, and next to realise the family's part within the community and the service that family can provide to the community. It is always important to remember, that though you may provide a service to the community you are never a servant and you are entitled to receive a service in return for that which you provided.

There is always enough for everyone when all are behaving within this awareness. It is when individuals exceed their spiritual purpose that difficulties occur. Again, we draw your attention to those two words, greed and power. The negative use of these energies, the energy of greed and the energy of power, act out through the ego. Within the body the ego seeks to be the power. It draws its energy from others, mainly through the tools of submission and dependency, and through ignorance or lack of awareness. It is hoped that through these writings you will regain your awareness and be neither submissive nor dependant. When all within a community gain this awareness and how it can unify those within its population, then the community has a power and place in the world as God Created it, in other words a paradise on Earth. The next quest will be to reunify the Elements."

REUNIFICATION.....

15.

"Naturally humankind cannot be expected to make the radical changes in its behaviour that would enable the process of reunification to commence. If one is to look about them, they will see the awareness of the necessity to change is all around them. You can see how the world of humankind is slowly destroying itself. Many seek to apportion the blame to others rather than to acknowledge the part they themselves are playing in this scenario of destruction. It's as simple as supply and demand. Humankind is demanding a more lazy way of living, to have 'things' that appear to offer them comfort and convenience. These latter come at a price, that price being the consumption of natural resources in a wasteful and unnatural way. This is unsustainable.

Humankind has taken over the role of creation. As it was created is not enough anymore. Humankind has lost its sense of its place on that planet. It sees itself as a separate species with Divine rights over everything else in that world. It sees itself as the superior species. It sees itself as having an intelligence that no other species has. It fails to see that in reality it has an ignorance that no other species has. It has an ego.

You will have heard of what are called, "The Seven Deadly Sins"? They are pride, covetous, lust, anger, gluttony, envy, and sloth. All these 'sins' are perpetrated through the human ego. It is in the area of these 'sins' that dependencies are created, and where humankind can be manipulated by those who exploit and control their fellow beings. Because the human race has been desensitised to the awareness of the wrong, they do, they are unconscious to the fact that they manifest these actions on a daily basis. Because of its unconsciousness it does not recognise what it has caused nor the effect it is having on humanity's spiritual life. Few can even recognise particular hungers they are feeling, for example most think that the only way to satisfy a hunger is to eat food, and whereas eating food only satisfies one form of hunger. Bad health is so often caused by this lack of sensitivity. Pain is treated in a manner that defeats its purpose; many seek to change their lives so that they can live with the pain, rather than change their lives so that there is no pain.

God didn't create fences, state boundaries, different religions, or different nationalities. There is only the species, amongst all different species, that is called the human race. It is sad to see that the members of that species fail to recognise that they are part of one great big family and work together as such. It is important to allow free flow of humanity across the planet and not have unnatural, manmade borders for them to be restricted by. If one was to remove the temptation of the seven sins there would be no difficulties. You will have experienced the refreshing visitation from someone from another family, from another parish, from another country? Where do you think the problems from

170

such a visit can arise? The answer is simple, the problems arise through your ego, one of the sins is triggered, and the results can lead to some un-human behaviour. The world has the capacity to cater for all inhabitants of all species. Nature will regulate the numbers. When humankind takes its proper place in that world, and stops interfering with nature, the whole system will self-regulate. When humankind once again realises that Creation is perfect and that incarnation through a physical body is a part of the eternal life of the Spirit, then perhaps humankind will stop its interference with nature.

It will be difficult for people to recognise that luxuries are not necessities. All the needs of human existence can be provided through the correct utilisation of nature. We will remind you that in the beginning Creation was perfect, and it still is to this day. The salvation of the human species, and indeed the salvation of all species, lies in the reversion of humankind to its God created nature, to living within the consciousness of spirituality. It is vital that this be recognised. The next step for humankind to take is the placing of everything in its life into a spiritual framework. It is only then that true love and compassion for one's fellow being can be experienced. It is only then that one can be of service to the collective humanity. Share and be shared with, love and be loved, provide and be provided for, be humble and avoid humiliation, accept and be accepted, respect and be respected, tolerate and be tolerated. There are so many qualities that the human has to enjoy from within themselves and from their fellows.

Your world can change immediately by you making one positive decision. It can change for the better. There are so many differing cultures in your world, each with its own unique qualities. It is only by embracing these other cultures that you can appreciate what those qualities have to offer you. As we started

171

this dissertation discussing the elements and their separation, maybe we should now look at concluding by discussing the reunification of those elements. The only two elements that have almost been totally destroyed are those of Air, and Water. You will see that when we look at these elements in physical terms rather than in energy terms, it is readily apparent how damaged they are. The continents ruled by these elements are suffering serious pollution and the resulting illnesses, both physical and mental are increasing. We see that humankind is at last giving cognisance to this condition but is unfortunately trying to resolve it while still trying to make financial profit and feeding greed. However, if you the individual play your part voluntarily, then you begin to supply rather than demand. If you begin to learn to rely on your own resources rather than depend on so-called authority to provide for you then you will have begun the journey of reunification. Those who follow you will then continue the journey. This can spread exponentially throughout the world. You will find then that those who have always been guardians of the other elements of Earth and Fire will assist Air and Water. The warriors will gather as one great force, all in harmony, and all in union. Peace will once again be restored, and the planet Earth will once again become paradise. It might happen faster than you might think. Why not start playing your part now by changing those habits that are, in light of this dissertation, shown to be destructive to the world of humanity."

Separation and Reunification of the Elements.

Separation and Reunification of the Elements.

Made in the USA
Middletown, DE
20 February 2021